KHAKI SHORTS AND SAFFRON FLAGS

Tapan Basu teaches in the Department of English at Hindu
College, Delhi University. Pradip Datta and Sambuddha Sen
teach in the Department of English at Shri Venkateswara
College, Delhi University. Sumit Sarkar is Professor of History at
Delhi University and Tanika Sarkar teaches in the Department of
History at St. Stephen's College, Delhi University.

TRACTS FOR THE TIMES

Editorial Board
S. Gopal • Romila Thapar

Editor
Neeladri Bhattacharya

ALSO IN THE SERIES

The Question of Faith
Rustom Bharucha

Environmental Consciousness and Urban Planning
M N Buch

Kashmir: Towards Insurgency
Balraj Puri

COVER: SUSETTA BOZZI

TRACTS FOR THE TIMES / 1

Khaki Shorts and Saffron Flags

A Critique of the Hindu Right

TAPAN BASU • PRADIP DATTA
SUMIT SARKAR • TANIKA SARKAR
SAMBUDDHA SEN

Orient Longman

KHAKI SHORTS AND SAFFRON FLAGS

Orient Longman Limited

Registered Office
3-6-272 Himayatnagar
Hyderabad 500 029 (A.P.)

Other Offices
Kamani Marg, Ballard Estate, Bombay 400 038
17 Chittaranjan Avenue, Calcutta 700 072
160 Anna Salai, Madras 600 002
1/24 Asaf Ali Road, New Delhi 110 002
80/1 Mahatma Gandhi Road, Bangalore 560 001
3-6-272 Himayatnagar, Hyderabad 500 029
Birla Mandir Road, Subzi Bagh, Patna 800 004
S.C. Goswami Road, Panbazar, Guwahati 781 001
"Patiala House", 16-A Ashok Marg, Lucknow 226 001

ISBN 0 86311 383 4

Published by
Orient Longman Limited
1/24 Asaf Ali Road
New Delhi 110 002

Typeset by
Scribe Consultants
B4/30 Safdarjung Enclave
New Delhi 110 029

Printed in India at
Rekha Printers Private Limited
A-102/1 Okhla Industrial Area Phase II
New Delhi 110 020

Contents

Contents

Editor's Preface

TRACTS FOR THE TIMES will attempt to provide meaningful information, critical perspectives, and theoretical reflections on various themes of contemporary concern. The tracts will seek to deepen our knowledge of crucial issues, query our common sense, re-think old concepts, and analyse the social and economic problems we confront.

This is a tract on the Hindu Right. Today, possibly more than any earlier time in the history of Independent India, we need to know about the communal forces which threaten to rupture Indian society. On December 6, 1992, the Babri Masjid was destroyed. This was not simply the consequence of spontaneous vandalism. Behind the action lies a long history of Hindutva politics which celebrates aggression and violence, declares war against other communities, and scorns at legal and democratic norms.

The events of December 6 and after re-affirm that the RSS and the VHP dictate the politics of the Hindu Right, they define the limits within which the Bharatiya Janta Party can maneuver. The Hindu right has for long operated with two faces; it has presented itself in two different ways. On the one hand it has sought to present a gentle face, symbolized in L.K. Advani's beatific smile; on the other it has widely projected an angry, aggressive and savagely sectarian face expressed in the speeches of Sadhvi Rithambara and Uma Bharati. These two faces are iconically represented, as this tract shows, in the twin images of Ram popularized through the posters and stickers of the VHP: the image of Ramlalla, the child god, and the image of Ram as the masculine warrior god. The Hindu Right also talks in two languages: the language of democracy and that of authoritarianism, the language of law and that of force. The BJP claims to function within a constitutional, democratic, legal framework; but the activities of the RSS, the VHP and the Bajrang Dal mock this framework. The politics of the Hindu Right derives its dynamic from the complex relationship between these seemingly opposing tendencies: from their complementarity and contradiction. December 6, 1992 revealed the sad logic of this politics. It revealed the hollowness of the BJP's democratic rhetoric and the ugly power of the violent forces of Hindutva.

This tract on the Hindu Right, written and printed before the Babri Masjid was destroyed, focuses on the RSS and the VHP. It allows us to reflect more meaningfully on the present, to locate the unfolding events within the longer history of communal mobilization.

The Rashtriya Swayamsevak Sangh claims to be a cultural, not a political, organization. Its object is to reform the Hindu self, to create a Hindu identity aware of its cultural heritage. This cultural project is, however, deeply political. It extends the reach of politics to every sphere of society. The RSS realizes that even sports can be an effective arena of politics. Through an involvement in games and physical exercises, the RSS seeks to create bonds of brotherhood and a sense of discipline amongst its cadres. This collectivity forged through leisure-time socialization is also structured in political ways. The stories told in the shakhas are always charged with communal meanings; the inculcated values of absolute loyalty—the submission of the self to the leader, the submergence of the individual to the community—create a basis of authoritarianism; martial training allows the possibility of a militarization of society. The communalization of society proceeds through a variety of other RSS cultural activities.

This tract explores in fascinating detail the history of the RSS, their organizational structure, the inner life of the shakhas, the RSS ideology of Hindutva, the seemingly invisible politics of sports and leisure, the communal use of cultural symbols and rituals, and the educational programmes of the shishu mandirs. It reveals the political implications of Savarkar's slogan 'Hinduize politics and militarize Hinduism'. It shows how the programme of 'Hinduization' involves a specific construction of Hindu self—a virile, masculine, aggressively communal self which is intolerant of other faiths, even of other conceptions of Hinduism.

From the RSS the discussion moves to the Vishwa Hindu Parishad. The tract analyses the history of the organization and its activities, its ideology and political rhetoric. It shows how the formation of the VHP in 1964 marks a new phase in the history of Hindutva. The VHP was specifically set up to forge a corporate Hindu identity, to unite all Hindu sects in opposition to Islam. The tract shows how communal cultural attitudes are constituted through stereotypes and symbols; how the VHP has used technology—video films, audio cassettes, stickers—to popularize the communal message; how it has mobilized women, youth and sadhus in a war against Muslims.

The authors end with a plea for an alternate secular culture. This appeal has an urgency at a time when the secular foundations of Indian society suddenly appear fragile. But this cultural project requires that we not only rethink the concepts and language of our secular discourse, but think of imaginative ways of constituting this secular culture.

Preface

Our book is primarily based on interviews conducted at Delhi, Khurja, Ayodhya, and parts of central UP, combined with a study of the publications and media products of the RSS, BJP and VHP. We are extremely grateful to the many who gave us their time and patience so generously at interviews. Biswamoy Pati made invaluable contributions in collecting and helping to write up material from Nizamuddin. Our information about Khurja was collected along with Uma Chakrabarti, Prem Chowdhuri, Zoya Hasan, and Kumkum Sangari. Arindam Sengupta accompanied two members of our team on two trips to central UP in 1989 and 1991. We are grateful to Sanjiv Kakkar, Aijaz Ahmad, Nilanjan Mukhopadhyaya, Ashok Bhattachargi, and Prabhu Mahapatra for information and advice. Neeladri Bhattacharya, who suggested to us the idea of this collective venture, and Romila Thapar have helped us enormously through their comments and criticism. The responsibility for errors and inadequacies remain with us alone.

THE AUTHORS

Preface

Our book is primarily based on interviews conducted at Delhi, Khurja, Ayodhya, and parts of central UP, combined with a study of the publications and media products of the RSS, BJP and VHP. We are extremely grateful to the many who gave us their time and patience so generously, at interviews. Biswamoy Pati made invaluable contributions in collecting and helping to write up material from Nizamuddin. Our information about Khurja was collected along with Uma Chakravarti, Prem Chowdhury, Zoya Hasan, and Kumkum Sangari. Anindita Sengupta accompanied two members of our team on two trips to central UP in 1989 and 1991. We are grateful to Sanjay Kaistha, Aijaz Ahmad, Nilanjan Mukhopadhyay, Ashok Bhattacharya, and Prabhu Mahapatra for information and advice. Neeladri Bhattacharya, who suggested to us the idea of this collective venture, and Romila Thapar have helped us enormously through their comments and criticism. The responsibility for errors and inadequacies remain with us alone.

THE AUTHORS

1

Introduction

The significance of the politics of Hindutva* in contemporary India is self-evident. What is not so obvious is the institutional ground-work that supports this movement: its long historical roots, the precise meaning and implications of its objectives. The frequent representations of Hindutva as a spontaneous mass movement in search of Hindu identity naturalizes and suppresses a whole history of meticulously organized efforts towards a Hindu Rashtra.

Over a long time we have got accustomed to equating commu-nalism largely with separatist trends among the minorities. A com-munalism that claims to represent the majority community has the tremendous advantage of being able to masquerade as democratic and national. In democracy, however, no majority is ever assumed to be permanent, or based on a single unchanging identity alone: a majority is constructed from issue to issue and can change from programme to programme. The majority that Hindutva claims to represent, on the other hand, is by definition, permanent, for it is constituted solely by the fact that 85 per cent of the population are, by census statistics, Hindu. The multiple identities within this cat-egory, of caste, sect, region, gender, class or belief, are sought to be erased, and the organized forces of Hindutva arrogate to themselves

---

* We use this term throughout not in the sense of Hinduism, but to indicate the contemporary communal organizations and movements that use this banner.

1

a proprietorial right to define what Hinduism means. Thus old temples can be destroyed to clear the way for the VHP *mandir* at Ayodhya. The community, further, is then elided into the country and nation, the Hindu Rashtra.

The homogenizing consequences of the claim to speak uniquely for a community defined by religious identity alone is present in all varieties of communalism, but only majority communalism can change the nature of the Indian polity, subverting the basic principles of democracy and secularism. Majority communalism, furthermore, has very obviously been on the offensive in recent years, and the vast majority of riot victims over the past decade have been Muslims (or, in 1984, Sikhs). At Meerut, Maliana, Delhi, Bhagalpur and many other places, the very meaning of communal riot changed into something very like genocide with official connivance. Riots have become integral to election strategy: a clear correlation can often be seen, for instance, between riot areas and constituencies where the BJP won in the recent elections.[1] We decided, therefore, to concentrate primarily in this project on majority communalism, on Hindutva, studied through certain structural aspects of the RSS-VHP-BJP combine. Within Hindutva we have attempted here to study its evolution from the RSS to the VHP mobilization on Ram, keeping in mind that it is the RSS which really constitutes the fountainhead of aggressive Hindu communalism. A subsequent tract, which we hope to bring out in the near future, will trace the specific interconnections between Hindutva and recent communal riots, through case studies of Nizamuddin (March 1990), Khurja (December 1990 – February 1991), and the Ayodhya *kar seva* movement (winter 1990–91). Our focus here has been on Delhi and parts of UP. The constraints of space and expertise forbade any attempt to be comprehensive: the Shiv Sena, for instance, has been left out entirely, along with other regional variations in Hindu communalism.

At the heart of Hindutva lies the myth of a continuous thousand-year old struggle of Hindus against Muslims as the structuring principle of Indian history. Both communities are assumed to have been homogeneous blocs—of Hindu patriots, heroically resisting invariably tyrannical, 'foreign' Muslim rulers. Every element in this myth has been demolished by historians. If the early Muslim kings

2

had been invaders, so presumably were the Aryans. Nor could a Muslim peasant or artisan be classified as a member of a 'Muslim' ruling class. Conversely, many Hindu princes and zamindars were demonstratively a part of this class, and the proportion of Hindus in the highest ranks of the Mughal administrative-cum-military service (*mansabdari*) reached its maximum levels under the 'bigoted' Aurangzeb, then engaged in wars with the Marathas and Sikhs.[2] If the Hindus alone (occasionally) had to pay the *jeziya*, there were other taxes for which only Muslim subjects were liable. There were many wars between Muslim and Hindu kings, but extremely few instances, prior to the nineteenth century, of what even dimly resembled the mass communal movements of today. Academic refutations have gone on, but myths persist and proliferate providing a simplistic, hand-me-down history to the layman. Modern secular historiography, still composed mainly in English, has a very limited reach in a subcontinent marked by mass illiteracy, generally poor and dated textbooks, and now, by the attempt of the VHP and BJP to dominate oral culture through the audio-visual media.

The essential point that requires emphasis is that prior to the communicational and economic integration of the last quarter of the nineteenth century, sharply-defined identities and animosities across large expanses of space had relatively little chance of development. There were occasional instances of local religious clashes, though these could as well be intra-Muslim or intra-Hindu: Shia-Sunni disputes, or conflicts between different Hindu castes or sects. Individual Muslim rulers at times wrecked places of worship or behaved intolerantly—just as ruling groups or members of other religious communities have done occasionally in India or elsewhere. But news of such an incident in Bengal, say, would take months, perhaps years, to reach Punjab or Malabar: today we get it within hours. It is not accidental, therefore, that broader identities of many types started getting consolidated roughly around the late nineteenth to the early twentieth century. What came to be termed a communal identity (Hindu, Muslim or Sikh) was formed alongside of, and often interpenetrated with regional, caste, class and 'national' loyalties.

The myth of the Muslim invader and Hindu resistance has also been deployed to prove that Hindutva represents the true, native

3

nationalism. It may be conceded that there is an area of overlap in ideas and personnel between Hindu communalism and mainstream nationalism. The communalism of the majority community, Nehru once pointed out, can easily pass off as national, while that of the minorities is quickly branded as separatist.[3] It is well known, for instance, that the myth of medieval 'Muslim tyranny' and Hindu (particularly Rajput, Maratha and Sikh) 'national' resistance was developed or endorsed in the late nineteenth century by many of the acknowledged founding fathers of Indian nationalism: Bankimchandra would only be the most obvious example of this phenomenon. Tilak's Ganpati and Shivaji *utsavs* worsened communal relations in Maharashtra, Congress leaders like Madan Mohan Malaviya or Lala Lajpat Rai were also active in the Hindu Mahasabha, there was a preponderance of Hindu imagery in much nationalist propaganda, and at local levels Congress and Hindu communal organizations often shared the same cadres till the late 1930s.

Yet a dividing line could be suggested, in logic if not always so clearly in practice. From the Moderates' exposure of colonial economic exploitation through the drain of wealth theory, down to 1947, mainstream nationalism always had British rule as its principle target for critique or for struggle. In mature, self-conscious communalism, however (whether Hindu or Muslim), there was a break in this crucial respect, with the other major religious community becoming the primary enemy. The history of the RSS, as we shall see, is particularly revealing in this respect. Despite its enviable organizational strength and discipline, the RSS had remained consistently aloof from all movements against foreign rule. Savarkar's early anti-British record is unimpeachable and heroic; it is difficult to make a similar statement about his activities in the mid-1920s, after he had evolved into the principal ideologue of Hindutva and become the leader of the Hindu Mahasabha. Mahasabha members of local bodies, legislatures and services were urged by Savarkar to 'stick to their posts and continue to perform their regular duties' during the 1942 movement, and his wartime slogan, 'Hinduize politics and militarize Hinduism' meant in practice a combination of virulent anti-Muslim propaganda and full collaboration with the British.[4]

Twentieth century communal tensions and identities have often

4

been explained as distorted expressions of socio-economic conflicts, and/or the result of political manipulation. Thus Muslim peasants confronted Hindu landlords in East Bengal and Malabar and Hindu traders and moneylenders in the Punjab, while in Uttar Pradesh a relatively privileged Muslim gentry faced Hindu peasants and traders. The other standard interpretation has been in terms of British divide-and-rule strategies. Currently fashionable theories of overwhelmingly dominant 'colonial discourse' have refurbished the second line of argument, replacing the conspiratorial by the structural. Western categories and modes of analysis (imposed via census operations, for instance) are held responsible for the cutting-up of Indian society into distinct, often mutually opposed blocs of religion, tribe or caste. The interpretations are helpful so far as they go: the specifics of many contemporary riots, for example, can be explained fairly well in terms of a combination of local socio-economic tensions and political or discursive machinations.

Yet many questions remain unanswered. Why do class tensions so often get 'distorted'; how and why do political manipulations succeed, and how and to what extent did colonial discourse really dominate the subcontinental mind? It may be observed that a notion of an all-powerful colonial discourse tends to cast Indians in the role of simple victims and exempt them from their own initiatives and agency. Nor is there a satisfactory explanation as to why communalism on the whole has been a growing dimension of subcontinental politics and culture precisely from the 1920s onwards. The worsened relations and riots of the 1890s and 1900s were followed fairly soon by the impressive Hindu-Muslim unity of the Lucknow Pact and Khilafat years. Yet no such major reversal of trends happened after the mid-1920s. Growing competition between political elites in the context of imminent decolonization may seem to provide a plausible, if partial, explanation for deepening conflicts down to 1947. But the much-reduced Muslim minority in post-Independence India cannot, by any objective criteria, be said to pose a political threat—and yet Hindu communalism today is stronger than ever before in its history.

Within the whole corpus of explanations for communalism, there has been little work on it as an ideological formation—that is, not just a set of ideas, but the elaboration of organizational structures

5

that embody and spread these in effective ways. The mid-1920s seem to have been particularly crucial for Hindu communalism from this point of view, for they saw a series of developments (which will be detailed later) that was epitomized by the publication of V.D. Savarkar's *Who Is a Hindu?* in 1923 and the foundation of the RSS in 1925. As we shall see, Savarkar was able to present Hindutva as a coherent and powerful pattern of concepts. And for more than sixty years now, the quiet but extremely effective 'cultural' work of the RSS has been spreading these ideas and emotions, till they seem to have been internalized into the common sense of certain social groups in large parts of the country.

An ideological formation, however, requires preconditions and roots, whether real or imagined. And an understanding of this pre-history of contemporary Hindutva is crucial, not only for purposes of research, but to also map the changes the RSS has wrought in a tradition they claim to be unchanging. The RSS and its 'family' have a habit of concealing their innovations under the guise of maintaining or reviving supposedly age-old traditions. The most spectacular instance of this phenomenon is the VHP, which uses the latest in media technology and political double-speak, with the professed aim of exalting a Puranic hero as the model of Hindu character. In their conversations with us, RSS and VHP leaders like K.S. Sudarshan and B.L. Sharma claimed a long chain of predecessors for the Hindutva of today: Dayanand, Vivekananda, even Gandhi, Tagore, Bhagat Singh and many others. If the Fascists and Nazis of Europe had appealed to the iconoclastic tendencies of youth through their talk of a new civilization, the RSS, which tries to catch its adherents even younger, tells its cadres to revere their elders and the past.

A key element of the RSS view of Hindu tradition is that of catholicity. K.S. Sudarshan, Assistant General Secretary of the RSS, talked about 'many flowers, one garland; many rivers, one ocean' in defining Hindu nationalism. Posed in this general way, the RSS idea of catholicity, to a less-than-discerning eye, could simultaneously lay claim to two different ideas of catholicity which have arisen from two distinct traditions. One is the political and cultural vision of early nationalism which saw India as a federation of different communities. This was a tradition that included the ideas of Sir Sayyid

Ahmed and Madan Mohan Malaviya, and was formulated as a programme in Bepinchandra Pal's vision of 'composite patriotism'. Hindus, Muslims, Christians and tribals would each preserve its distinctive features and by cultivating them contribute to the common national life of India.'[5] Such views at times implied a socially conservative clinging to past traditions, and could offer a springboard for mutually opposed communal solidarities. This danger prompted a more radical reformulation of catholicity by Rabindranath Tagore from 1907 onwards. His ideal too was a 'unity in diversity', but this was to be the future-oriented unity of a *mahajati* based on an open and self-critical commingling of a variety of cultures, not of a federation of static traditionalist blocs.

The Hindutva which has developed from the 1920s, while often trying to appropriate the same language of unity in diversity, restricts the permitted variety within the bounds of Hindu traditions. All the flowers in Sudarshan's discourse make up the single garland of Hindutva, the many rivers flow into the one Hindu ocean. Sudarshan sharply distinguished the ideal of the RSS from any notion of 'composite culture'. The country can have only one Hindu culture, he declared, and so all must accept Ram—if not as divine, at least as the nation's hero.

Present-day Hindutva seems to be somewhat more closely related to another tradition of catholicity, which became widespread in the late nineteenth century. This was a catholicity bound up with what was called *adhikar-bheda*. According to this idea, each level or group within the vast hierarchy that is Hinduism should legitimately have its own distinct rituals and beliefs, and thus enormous diversity could be reconciled within an overruling Hindu solidarity. This idea was most closely associated with Ramakrishna, the nineteenth century religious leader who is approvingly cited by Golwalkar in his *Bunch of Thoughts*. However, Golwalkar's reverence seems misplaced, for Ramakrishna, drawing upon village traditions of tolerance and syncretism from which he had emerged, had imparted a unique range to this catholicity when he had declared that Hindu notions of divinity differ no more from Muslim or Christian than *jal* does from *pani* (both names denoting water in different tongues). Vivekananda, a name frequently cited by contemporary advocates of Hindutva, represents a slightly less unfair appropriation. The alleged

7

unique tolerance of Hinduism was transformed by Vivekananda into an argument for its consequent superiority over all other faiths. From the Chicago address of 1893 onwards, Vivekananda became a kind of roving ambassador for a fundamentally unified, muscular Hinduism. 'Our religion is truer than any other religion because it never conquered, because it never shed blood,' and today its adherents have to acquire 'iron muscles and nerves of steel.' Yet Vivekananda could also be a trenchant critic at times of high caste domination and gender oppression, and even prophesied a day when, the *sadhus* and Brahmins who 'suck the blood of poor people' would be displaced by a 'rising of the Shudra class'.[6] The complacent, aestheticized contemplation of any number of oppressive practices as so many flowers in a garland, characteristic of today's Hindutva, would have been utterly foreign to Vivekananda and his capacity for self-criticism.

Hindutva's uncritical celebration of diversity represents a departure also from the tenets and practices of Dayanand, another frequently-cited father figure, who had founded the Arya Samaj through militant campaigns against priestly corruption and superstition. The linkages with subsequent Arya practices, however, are fairly close. Dayanand in his last years tempered reformist zeal with a growing emphasis upon Hindu unity, foregrounding cow protection and replacement of Urdu by Hindi in the Devanagri script: the two issues which underlay the worsening of communal relations in north India during the last two decades of the nineteenth century. Conflicts with orthodox Sanatan Dharma Sabha groups, extremely bitter in the earlier years, gradually died down, and the Arya Samaj came to contribute greatly in course of time to the cause of Hindutva in Punjab and UP.

Modern Hindutva really comes into its own with V.D. Savarkar's definition of the Hindu in 1923 as 'a person who regards the land of *Bharatvarsha* from Indus to the Seas as his Fatherland, as well as his Holy land—that is the cradle land of his religion.' The implications of this *pitribhumi-punyabhumi* equation are brought out in course of the pamphlet *Hindutva/ Who is a Hindu?* in a formidably lucid manner. Ascribing sanctity to the land of one's birth is a standard patriotic rhetoric, and Savarkar's bid to link up with the nationalist discourse was strengthened by the fact that the pamphlet had been drafted in the Andaman cellular jail. At the same time, the definition is wielded in a firmly exclusionist manner. The patriotism of Indian Muslims and Christians is always inferior and suspect, for, with holy lands in Arabia and Palestine, they cannot identify *pitribhumi* uniquely with *punyabhumi*. The argument is eminently extendable, and Golwalkar, predictably, brought in the Communists in his *Bunch of Thoughts*. If need be, advocates of secularism, science and democracy can all be tarred with the same brush, for all these ideals had developed initially in the modern West. Exclusion, however, goes along with a supreme internal catholicity. All differences of ritual, belief, and caste are irrelevant: what matters is not content, but origin in (a vaguely and arbitrarily defined) *Bharatvarsha*. Monists, monotheists, polytheists and atheists, Sikhs, Arya Samajists, and advocates of Sanatan Dharma, are all equally good Hindus for Savarkar. Again, if differences and tensions of caste, say, are unimportant, nothing needs to be done about such contradictions, the important thing is Hindu solidarity.

Savarkar soars above sectarian and ritual differences within what he has defined as the fold of Hindutva, but there is also a reverse, downward movement in his discourse. No particular Hindu symbol or rite is indispensable, but since Hindutva involves reverence for a 'common culture', 'common civilization', and 'history', any of these can be taken up in a pragmatic manner and resanctified. And so Diwali, Rakhi and Hindu pilgrimages are discovered to be essential 'from a national and racial point of view'. Muslims and Christians who do not accept these once again become suspect: 'their names and their outlook smack of foreign origin'. Particularly significant in today's context is Savarkar's handling of the Ram symbol: 'Some of us worship Ram as an incarnation, some admire him as a hero and a warrior, all love him as the most illustrious representative monarch of our race.'

Savarkar established the fundamental pattern of ideas, in this pamphlet initially published under the pseudonym 'A Mahratta'. Two years later, a fellow Maharashtrian, K.B. Hedgewar, undertook the task of providing the essential organizational backup by founding the RSS at Nagpur. The timing of these two developments is significant, and so is their common location in Maharashtra.

The immediate context for the initiative of Savarkar and

Hedgewar was obviously provided by the massive communalization of Indian political life during the mid-1920s. The weakening, and eventual collapse, of the Congress-Khilafat alliance after Gandhi's unilateral withdrawal of the Non-cooperation Movement in February 1922 was followed by an unprecedented wave of riots. They ranged from Kohat in the NWFP to Dacca, and there were no less than 91 communal outbreaks between 1923 and 1927 in UP, the worst-affected province. The Arya Samaj under Shraddhanand started a purificatory-cum-organizational drive (*shuddhi* and *sangathan*) to win back low caste groups whose practices had incorporated Islamic elements: the Muslim communal counterparts of these movements were *tabligh* (propaganda) and *tanzim* (organization). *Shuddhi* had been formulated by the Arya Samaj, already in Dayanand's time, as a device for countering Christian, and later Sikh and Muslim, proselytizing. Since conversions were most common among low castes and untouchables, Shraddhanand in the early 1920s sought to develop *shuddhi* into a strategy for tackling untouchability. His pamphlet *Hindu Sangathan: Saviour of A Dying Race* (1926) combined the themes of alleged Hindu population decline due to conversions, and the consequent need to end untouchability if the 'dying race' was to be saved. There is much in this pattern, as we shall see, that anticipates current VHP methods of dealing with caste discrimination in ways that do not eliminate, but ultimately strengthen, high caste hegemony. The Mahasabha quickly endorsed Savarkar's 'catholic' definition of Hindutva, and its Benaras session (August 1923) called for the organization of Hindu self-defence squads. The Mahasabha was, and remained, little more than an annual conference—but Hindu communalism was now in search for disciplined cadres.

The centrality of Maharashtra in the formation of the ideology and organization of Hindutva in the mid-1920s might appear rather surprising, as Muslims here were a small minority and hardly a threat, and there had been no major riots in this region during the early 1920s. But Maharashtra had witnessed a powerful anti-Brahmin movement of backward castes from the 1870s onwards, when Jyotiba Phule had founded his Satyashodhak Samaj. By the 1920s, the Dalits, too, had started organizing themselves under Ambedkar. Hindutva in 1925 as in 1990–91, was an upper caste

10

bid to restore a slipping hegemony: RSS' self image of its own history, we shall see shortly, makes this abundantly clear. There was, in addition, the distrust felt for the new Gandhian Congress on the part of a section of the predominantly Chitpavan Brahmin Tilakites. It is symptomatic that B.S. Moonje, an old associate of Tilak, was one of the five who founded what became the RSS on Vijaya Dashami day, 1925.

NOTES

1. Uma Chakravarty *et al.*, 'Communalization of Khurja', *The Hindu*, 17 June 1991. Also Chakravarty, *et al.*
2. M. Athar Ali, *Mughal Nobility under Aurangzeb*, Bombay, 1966.
3. Nehru's speech at the AICC, 11 May 1958, quoted in A.C. Noorani, 'BJP: Child of RSS and Heir to Hindu Mahasabha', *Mainstream*, 27 July 1991.
4. V.D. Savarkar, *Historic Statements*, Bombay, 1967.
5. Bepinchandra Pal, *Shivaji Utsava*, 1906.
6. Swami Vivekananda, *Collected Works* (9th ed., Calcutta, 1964), Vol. III, pp. 274–5; *Letters of Swami Vivekananda* (Calcutta, 1970), p. 81.

2

A Sketch of RSS History

DR. HEDGEWAR'S RSS

Let Muslims look upon Ram as their hero and the communal problems will be all over...

Organiser, 20 June 1971.

The above quotation from the official weekly of the RSS is refreshingly candid in its avowal of a Hindu intolerance and aggressiveness quite unconnected with any real or imagined Muslim intransigence. It is also revealingly indicative of the long history behind the seemingly spontaneous and popular contemporary movement for the 'liberation' of the Ram Janambhoomi complex at Ayodhya. The war cry for this 'liberation' was articulated by the Vishwa Hindu Parishad (VHP) only in late 1983, and taken up subsequently by fraternal organizations like the Bharatiya Janata Party (BJP) or the Bajrang Dal (BD). The leaders and activists of these and similar organizations however freely acknowledge the RSS as 'the mother of us all'. *'Gun jo hai, sab uske hai, dosh hoga to hamara hoga,'* declared B.L. Sharma, then Secretary of the Indraprastha unit of the VHP and now BJP MP from East Delhi, in an interview given to some of us in April 1990.

Ram has been central to the RSS 'cultural' project right from its inception in 1925. Dr. K.B. Hedgewar deliberately chose Vijaya Dashami for its inauguration, the day on which Ram was supposed to have defeated Ravana in that epic conflict between good and evil

12

which is the substance of the *Ramayana*. The infant organization was given its name in 1927 on Ram Navami—popularly believed to be the birthday of Ram—and the saffron flag adopted on the same day, the *bhagwa jhanda*, was supposed to be the flag of Ram in its colour and shape. Thus from the very beginning the RSS has used the legends of Ram to define its ideology, its peculiar brand of 'culture'. The confrontation over Ram clearly presaged by the *Organiser* has been perceived by the RSS for at least two decades now as a crucial milestone in the achievement of its long-cherished goal of making India into a Hindu Rashtra. As Achin Vanaik has accurately observed,

> It is not the VHP or the BJP or the Bajrang Dal or the Bharatiya Mazdoor Sangh or the Akhil Bharatiya Vidyarthi Parishad that is the main driving force of Hindu Rashtra. It is the RSS.[1]

Yet the RSS has generally shunned publicity, preferring to work in a quiet, unostentatious, 'cultural' manner, training up the cadres for the other, more flamboyant members of its affiliated organizations, what the adherents call its 'family'. Of course, as we shall substantiate in the course of this chapter, the RSS insistence that its work lies in the propagation of Hindu culture alone without any political overtones, is just a play with words. The notion of Hindu culture that is propagated in its *shakhas* is a definition of a majoritarian and authoritarian *rashtra* where Hindus, under RSS direction, will lay down the rules by which the minorities must abide. Its version of Hindu culture is inextricably mingled with antagonism against the non-Hindu.

This shunning of publicity has helped to produce a strange relative silence about the RSS even in much secular writing. To take two recent examples: Hedgewar and the RSS get a couple of lines, and no index reference, in Gyan Pandey's *Construction of Communalism in Colonial North India* (Delhi, 1990), and even the collection of essays on the Ayodhya dispute, edited by S. Gopal *Anatomy of Confrontation* (Delhi 1991) contains little about this core organization of Hindu communalism. We therefore decided to focus first of all on the RSS, present a sketch of its foundation and history, to be followed by an analysis of the organizational structure through

13

which it has been able to give birth to a whole series of 'family' members.

Material produced by the RSS itself, or by writers fairly sympathetic towards it (like Anderson and Damle), along with some interviews with activists prominent in the RSS or its 'family', perforce became our major source.[2] This is not necessarily a disadvantage, however, for critical analysis of such material permits a simultaneous focus on present-day perceptions of the RSS of its own past, the way in which it selectively uses or invests it as a resource in its activities today. Such use is peculiarly vital for an ideology and organization which, as we have seen, emphasizes continuities and ancestors.

Our study of the RSS'construction of its own origins may begin most appropriately with Dr. Hedgewar himself:

As a result of the Non-Cooperation Movement of Mahatma Gandhi the enthusiasm [for nationalism] in the country was cooling down and the evils in social life which that movement generated were menacingly raising their head. As the tide of national struggle came to ebb mutual ill-will and jealousies came on the surface. Personal quarrels raged all round. Conflicts between various communities had started. Brahmin-non-Brahmin conflict was nakedly on view. No organisation was integrated or united. The *yavan*-snakes reared on the milk of Non-Cooperation were provoking riots in the nation with their poisonous hissing.[3]

An official publication of the RSS gives the following account of its origins:

A change was coming over the country. The aftermath of the 1921 movement had come to Doctorji (Hedgewar) as a shock. Indian Muslims had proved themselves Muslims first and Indians only secondarily so that when the Khilafat was given up in Turkey, they withdrew from the allied movement for national independence. The whole atmosphere was charged with Muslim fanaticism. 'Allah ho akbar' and not 'Bharat mata ki jai' was heard everywhere. Soon there were Muslim riots in Bannu, Kohat, Multan, Nagpur, Kanpur and elsewhere. 'These are not Hindu-Muslim riots,' he would say 'These are

14

Muslim riots because in every single case it is they who start them and go on the offensive.' These riots culminated in the Moplah atrocity, completed with arson, loot, murder, rape and forced conversion. The nation was dazed. And Doctorji wondered: 'Is it Khilafat (restoration of Khalif) or Akhilafat (catastrophe for all)?...' It became evident that the Hindus were the nation in Bharat and that Hindutva was Rashtriyatva. While wishful thinkers pretended not to see the writing across the national political firmament, the realist in Dr. Hedgewar refused to dream up wishy-washy dreams. The truth was out. Only Hindus would free Hindustan and they alone could save Hindu culture. Only Hindu strength could save the country. There was no escape from the logic of facts. Hindu youth had to be organised on the basis of personal character and absolute love of the motherland. There was no other way. The agony of the great soul expressed itself in the formation of the Rashtriya Swayamsevak Sangh. With five friends he started the day-to-day programme of RSS. The great day was the auspicious Vijaya Dashami day of 1925.[4]

The accounts are revealing in a number of different ways. The Non-Cooperation upsurge, highest point in anti-British unity in the entire history of modern Indian nationalism, is unequivocally condemned. The 'yavan snakes', it seems, are at their most dangerous when they are fighting foreign rule side by side with the Hindus, when they cease behaving in the expected 'anti-national' manner. Hindu-Muslim fraternity is dangerous because the ideal, evidently is not a united, free India but a 'Hindu Rashtra'—only Hindus could constitute 'the nation in Bharat'. This is hard-headed 'realism'—a style of argument much favoured throughout by Hindu communalists. Yet the stereotype of the Muslim as anti-national has to be preserved, and so history must be doctored. Khilafatists are blamed for withdrawing from the 'allied movement', though it was Gandhi and the Congress leadership which had unilaterally called off that movement in 1922. The catalogue of riots is similarly twisted, to present the Moplah rebellion—actually far more of a peasant rising against landlords than a straightforward communal disturbance—as a culmination (it had in reality preceded the other riots that had been listed by several years). And Hedgewar's account clearly reveals the centrality for him of the Brahmin-non-Brahmin conflict. Organized Hindutva emerges right from the beginning as an upper caste reaction to efforts at self-assertion by downtrodden groups within the Hindu fold.

RSS literature tends to exaggerate the role, greatness, and originality of Hedgewar. The four others present at the inaugural Vijaya Dashami meeting—Dr. B.S. Moonje, Dr. L.V. Paranjpe, Dr. B.B. Thalkar and Baburao Savarkar (V.D. Savarkar's brother)—are seldom named in such publications, probably because all of them then belonged to the Hindu Mahasabha, an organization with which the RSS's relations have not always been particularly friendly. In addition, they were leaders of the Hindu Swayamsevak Samiti and Hindu Samrakshan Samiti—volunteer groups set up by the Nagpur Hindu Mahasabha after a riot in that city in 1923. There had clearly been some anticipation of the RSS type of organization in Nagpur itself before the 1925 meeting, and the idea did not simply float down from heaven into Hedgewar's head, as subsequent RSS accounts would like us to believe.

Hedgewar's true originality lay in his brilliant elaboration of a suggestion first made by Sister Nivedita (an indebtedness which the RSS today is proud to acknowledge, for it strengthens its nationalist credentials): 'Congregate and pray together for fifteen minutes, every day, and Hindu society will become an invincible society.'[5] This was developed in course of time into a single format of rituals-cum-physical training, to be performed at identical times by RSS branches (*shakhas*) all over the country. The notion of a spiritual energy generated by universal, time-bound prayer and ritual draws its inspiration from a concept of an invisible congregation.

The Vijaya Dashami meeting analysed the weakness of existing Hindu organizations in Nagpur city. Very significantly, the main problem was felt to lie in the dependence of literate upper caste Hindus on the lower castes in times of actual combat. The educated Hindu, the meeting decided, must give up such dependence and learn combat skills himself—a revealing admission of the felt unreliability of low castes, evidently in the context of sharpening Brahmin-non-Brahmin conflict. The RSS, from its inception down to today, has been overwhelmingly middle class Brahmin or Bania

16

n composition, drawn together on the basis of a fear psychosis directed against other social groups: Muslims, most overtly, but by implication also lower caste Hindus.

Hedgewar and his associates decided to concentrate on teenage boys, as grown-up men were often too corrupted, or preoccupied by family concerns, to be relied upon. There is a link here with the practices of revolutionary terrorist organizations, which too recruited heavily from schoolboys and college youth—while a religious leader like Ramakrishna had similarly drawn most of his intimate disciples from teenagers. The training of the boys would combine physical culture with inculcation of a sense of the greatness of Hindu traditions. Hedgewar was given sole charge of this training programme, and he carefully began to recruit schoolboys from the twelve-to-fifteen year age group, scrutinizing their eligibility in terms of capacity for loyalty and obedience. He was developing a group loyal to him personally, a militant coterie which would not stand duality of allegiance either to persons or to principles. Recruitment in very early youth must have helped to preserve unquestioning loyalty. Association from early boyhood creates a peer group that would last a lifetime and would share memories of growing up together as well as identical convictions. The cohesiveness of the group would then be rooted in exceptionally strong emotional and political ties. A vacant plot of land in the city—where now stands Hedgewar Bhawan, headquarters of the RSS—was cleaned up by the boys themselves under Hedgewar's leadership and made into a playground-cum-training area, and here the *shakha* programme began, in early 1926. As yet the organization had no name, flag, or other formal rituals, funds or hierarchy: it was still a purely local affair. Hedgewar personally supervised the physical training, and as an intellectual exercise, told and retold stories of Hindu heroes like Shivaji and Rana Pratap who had fought Muslims valiantly in the past. He also deepened his personal contact with the boys by taking them out for picnics and sports and, unlike many other superficially similar volunteer groups, refused to employ his boys to do small chores for organizations dominated by others. This gave Hedgewar's boys a sense of self-importance and independence. They felt superior to other volunteers: prepared to do anything for themselves or their leader; they were at nobody else's beck and call.

On Ram Navami day, 1926, the infant organization, after con
siderable discussion between Hedgewar and his co-founders, gav
itself the name of Rashtriya Swayamsevak Sangh. Hedgewar insisted
on the term *rashtriya* (national) for his exclusively Hindu organi
zation, for he wanted to re-assert the identity of Hindu with *rash
triya*. A flag was chosen that allegedly belonged to Ram, and wa
said to have been used by Shivaji. A prayer, in mixed Hindi and
Marathi, would be sung at the end of every *shakha* meeting, along
with the slogans of *Rashtra guru Samarth Ramdas ki jai* and *Bhara
Mata ki jai*. The prominence of Shivaji, his flag, and his guru Ram
das in RSS ritual gave it a strongly Maharashtrian complexion, lead
ing even to rumours that its aim was a Peshwa restoration.

Between April and June 1927, the RSS held a training camp fo
twenty *swayamsevaks* (volunteers). There was training in the use o
lathi (staff), sword, javelin and dagger—weapons, it may be noted
which could be helpful in a street brawl with unarmed fellow In
dians, but were of little use in fighting British soldiers or police
men. The boys played indigenous games like *kabaddi* and *kho kho
and heard lectures on Hindu nationalism, the disloyalty of non-Hin
dus,[2] the fultlity of Gandhian methods and the past heroism of th
Hindus. The constantly reiterated message was that the Hindu
were suffering because they had become unorganized, liberal, gen
erous and peaceable. They needed to become militant and powerful
and for that an organization like the RSS was essential.

1927 was the year when the flagging national movement had
started to revive, with a powerful agitation against the all-white
Simon Commission, with the establishment of patriotic student and
youth organizations, the beginnings of a working class upsurge, and
with growing pressures within the Congress for the adoption o
complete independence as its goal. From all such developments the
RSS kept itself strictly aloof, even though Hedgewar personally re
mained reasonably active in the Congress. The first training camp
apart, 1927 is important in RSS history for the major role it played
in a communal riot in Nagpur in September 1927. The riot wa
followed by a rapid spread of RSS organization in and around Nag
pur.

Once again, the RSS version of this incident given by C.P

Bhishikar will repay close attention. Bhishikar begins with a comment about general Muslim aggressiveness, and then goes on:

> Stones were thrown at Doctorji's house. He was also receiving letters threatening to kill him. Tension was growing in the atmosphere. And the Muslims hatched a conspiracy to bring out a massive procession on September 4, 1927 (Mahalakshmi Puja day) and indulge in rioting. The procession was scheduled for the afternoon, a time during which Hindus would be resting after lunch. The Sangh workers got wind of the plan, and knew that the procession was going to be attended by riot. Doctorji was personally out of Nagpur on that day. The procession was to pass through the Mahl area, an educated middle class locality. On both sides of the route there were a number of narrow lanes. The processionists were equipped with *lathis*, javelins, knives, daggers. Those who wanted to indulge in violence and loot indulged in thunderous slogans of 'Allah ho akbar' and 'din din' and attacked a house situated in one of the narrow lanes. But at the entrance itself they got a thorough beating. Thereafter they got thrashing at every lane entrance. Several rioters had their heads broken. The procession broke up and people began to run. The fleeing *goondas* (hooligans) beat up the lone Hindus they found in the way. After the first retaliation against the Muslim intrusion several Hindus left their lunch unfinished in anger and came out; by the evening they beat back the invaders. For three days thereafter stray incidents continued. The atmosphere remained tense but not a single Hindu locality was attacked. The Hindu society showed a unity and militancy which inspired self-confidence.[6]

The incident is worthy of such a long and detailed description, the author adds, because it won for the RSS the confidence of the community and ushered in a new era of RSS work in Nagpur and other parts of the Central Provinces.

The Nagpur clash and, even more, Bhishikar's style of narration provide a vivid case study of a riot and the self-justificatory communal discourse that develops around it. The Muslims are depicted as aggressors, and some of them may well have had violent designs.

But the hard facts indicated in the RSS account itself are that the procession did not really clash with any Hindu ceremonial (this being the time for a Hindu gentleman's siesta), and that the Muslims got a 'thorough beating at every lane entrance'. Thus, in a pattern that repeats itself right down to today, reassertion of the basic tenet of Muslim aggressiveness is delicately balanced by an emphasis upon successful (because militant and organized) Hindu 'self-defence'. In a similar equipoise, the RSS's own role is both kept in the background, and yet subtly displayed. The incident had been preceded by an RSS camp, the *swayamsevaks* had somehow 'got wind of the plot', there were evidently young men ready to fight at every lane entrance. But no details are given of RSS preparation, and the leader himself was out of town. Formal connections between the riot and the RSS would be difficult to establish, but there is no doubt at all that it was the RSS which gained most from it. The whole pattern is tediously, even frighteningly familiar. In post-Independence India too, the RSS always brands charges of its involvement in communal riots as motivated propaganda by 'pseudo-secularists'. Yet at least three commissions of inquiry—Reddy, Vythayathil, Venugopal—have found RSS inspiration behind anti-Muslim and anti-Christian riots, not so much in direct cadre participation, but through long-term and sustained communal propaganda.[7]

The Nagpur riot vastly enhanced RSS prestige, for the word spread around that a hundred Hedgewar boys had successfully repulsed a violent Muslim mob. Hedgewar was quick to consolidate the gains. In March 1928, an oath was instituted for *swayamsevaks* to intensify their commitment through a romantic aura that was also reminiscent of revolutionary-terrorist traditions. Members henceforward had to pledge their lives to the cause of the RSS and the Hindu Nation. Hedgewar's speech at the first oath-taking ceremony (31 March 1928) once again used the symbolism of Ram, for its leitmotif was the famous passage in Tulsidas: 'Life itself can be sacrificed but the plighted word cannot be betrayed.' He also started inviting well-known personalities (like Vithalbhai Patel, the Speaker of the Central Assembly) to visit RSS camps, seeking to impress them through a display of the discipline of his boys. Meanwhile the first steps were being taken to spread the RSS beyond Maharashtra. Three *swayamsevaks* were sent to the Benaras Hindu

University as students to start an RSS unit there. Well-to-do sym-
pathisers apparently provided financial support, and Madan Mohan
Malaviya proved extremely helpful and provided Hedgewar's students with a premise where they could start their RSS office.

Expansion had its problems, however, for there were signs that
the *shakhas* under their *sanghchalaks* (directors) were at times pulling
in different directions, in the absence of a clear-cut hierarchy of
functionaries. In 1929 Anna Sohni, who had evolved the RSS system
of physical training, left the organization, in the first of a number
of internal clashes about which the RSS has always been extremely
secretive. A meeting of prominent RSS workers at Nagpur on 9–10
November 1929 decided to formalize the institutional structure.
The key principle adopted was that of *ek chalak anuvartita* (following
one leader), and, as proposed by Appaji Joshi, Hedgewar was chosen
as *sarsanghchalak*, supreme director on a life-time basis. Thus the
RSS decided to avoid internal democracy, and opted for a totally
centralized command structure, which Hedgewar would be free to
expand and elaborate as and when required. V.V. Kelkar explained
to the meeting that *ek chalak anuvartita* was on the lines of the
traditional Hindu joint family system and hence most appropriate
for an organization wedded to the rejuvenation of the Hindu way
of life. Dictatorial principles of organization have not been rare in
movements working underground, like Indian revolutionary-terrorist groups: the peculiarity of the RSS decision of 1929 was that it
was being taken by an organization which had no intention at all
of fighting militantly against British rule.

In December 1929, the Lahore Congress adopted Purna Swaraj
as the national goal, and Jawaharlal Nehru's presidential address
gave a new revolutionary dimension to the nationalist project by
placing it in the context of the international struggle against impe-
rialism. Three months later Gandhi started his Dandi march and
the Civil Disobedience Movement was born. The RSS, as usual,
remained deafeningly silent—except for a single, though interesting, circular issued by Hedgewar as *sarsanghchalak* concerning the
Congress decision to observe 26 January 1930 as Independence Day.
The circular audaciously claimed that 'the Indian National Congress
too has adopted our goal of Independence.' RSS *shakhas* should
therefore celebrate Independence Day—but through 'worship' of

21

'the national flag, that is, the *bhagwa jhanda*'. Not, it needs to be noted, the tricolour. 1930, in any case, remained the only year when the RSS celebrated 26 January, even though such celebration became a standard feature of the freedom movement, and often came to mean violent confrontation with the colonial police. The RSS preferred to conserve its martially-trained cadres for other objectives.

Hedgewar personally joined the satyagraha movement, and briefly went to jail, but otherwise the Civil Disobedience of 1930–31 is a non-event in RSS history. RSS expansion was resumed from 1931, particularly 1933–34, moving in tandem, it may be noted, with the decline of the national upsurge. The Congress was becoming worried by the drift of some of its members towards the RSS, and the latter's connections in these years with the Hindu Mahasabha, a rival political formation, added to these suspicions. In 1933 the Congress leader Jamnalal Bajaj sought clarifications about RSS attitudes on national issues from Hedgewar. Despite Hedgewar's efforts to allay suspicions through a personal meeting with Bajaj, the Congress in June 1934 passed a resolution forbidding its members from joining the RSS, the Hindu Mahasabha, and the Muslim League.

The RSS at this time did not want to make a demonstrative break with the nationalist mainstream. In December 1934 Hedgewar invited Gandhi to visit a camp at Wardha. K.S. Sudarshan in his interview claimed that Gandhi had been deeply impressed, and RSS sources describe the meeting with Hedgewar as an exchange of views between equals. 'There is no question of scoring points in such meetings. Leaders who talk with mutual confidence and goodwill try to understand each others point of view and to remove misunderstandings, if any...'[8] Gandhi's attitude towards the RSS in 1934 may have been somewhat noncommittal, but against this we need to place his unqualified denunciation of the organization some years later, which has been recorded by his secretary Pyarelal. In the wake of the 1946 riots, a member of Gandhi's entourage had praised the efficiency, discipline, courage and capacity for hard work shown by RSS cadres at Wagah, a major transit camp for Punjab refugees. 'But don't forget,' answered Gandhi, 'even so had Hitler's Nazis and the Fascists under Mussolini.' He went on to characterize the RSS

22

as a 'communal body with a totalitarian outlook'.[9] Gandhi categorically declared that 'the way [to national independence] does not lie through *akhadas*...if they are meant as a preparation for self-defence in Hindu-Muslim conflicts, they are foredoomed to failure. Muslims can play the same game, and such preparations, covert or overt, do cause suspicion and irritation. They can provide no remedy.'[10]

RSS relations with the Hindu Mahasabha during the 1930s kept fluctuating, but for some years were, on the whole, mutually fruitful. In 1931 Baburao Savarkar, who had founded a Tarun Hindu Sabha as the youth wing of the Mahasabha, merged his organization with the RSS. Lacking trained cadres of its own, the Mahasabha, too, had started regarding the RSS as an extension of its politics in the sphere of the youth. The Delhi session of the Hindu Mahasabha (1932) passed a resolution commending the activities of the RSS and emphasizing the need to spread its network all over the country. In the same year, the Mahasabha leader Bhai Parmanand extended a special invitation to Hedgewar to attend the Karachi session of the Hindu Yuvak Parishad, and the RSS leader was thus able to establish contacts with youth groups in Sindh and Punjab. Baburao Savarkar brought the RSS in touch with Mahasabha activists in Benaras and Delhi, and the great prestige of the Savarkar family among the upper castes of western Maharashtra enabled a major expansion of the RSS into that region. Pune developed into a kind of second headquarters for the RSS, and an additional training camp was started there from 1935, along with the main Nagpur camp. V.D. Savarkar, after his release from jail in 1937, also helped to enhance RSS prestige in Maharashtra by demonstratively visiting and speaking at *shakha* meetings. In 1940, Shyamaprasad Mukherjee, prominent Mahasabha leader, addressed a Lahore RSS *shakha* and declared that the organization was 'the one silver lining in the cloudy sky of India'.[11] Above all, it was the Mahasabha connection which enabled the RSS to start penetrating Hindi speaking northern India, today the principal base for itself and its affiliated organizations.

Yet there remained points of tension in the relations between the RSS and the Hindu Mahasabha. They culminated in an open breach after Golwalkar succeeded Hedgewar as *sarsanghchalak*. An early indication was the career of Nathuram Godse, future assassin of

Gandhi, who joined the RSS in 1930, and rapidly became a prominent speaker and organizer. Godse accompanied Hedgewar and Baburao Savarkar in an extended tour of western Maharashtra in 1932. Two years later, however, Godse deserted the RSS for the Hindu Mahasabha, apparently because 'Hedgewar refused to make the RSS a political organization.'[12]

Apart from the natural rivalries between two bodies with broadly similar aims but distinct organizational structures, there was this 'cultural'/'political' tension, which in fact has been a recurrent theme in RSS history. The Hindu Mahasabha was self-confessedly a political party, trying to project itself as an alternative to the Congress immersed mainly in elections and ministry-making. Hedgewar wanted his RSS to remain primarily 'cultural', pursuing more long term goals through quiet but sustained physical-cum-ideological training of cadres.

The expansion of the RSS was particularly rapid between 1937 and 1940, in the context of worsening Hindu-Muslim relations in northern India. Organizers were sent into Punjab, Delhi, the United Provinces and Bihar, and in 1939 Hedgewar decided to strike out for an all-India composition by sending *swayamsevaks* to Madras city, Tamil Nadu and Karnataka. There were 400 RSS centres with 40,000 members in 1938; by 1940, according to an RSS spokesman the number of volunteers had shot up to 100,000. Significantly however the focus remained entirely on towns, and, within them on recruiting from 'university students and shopkeepers and clerk of the lower middle classes'.[13]

As the RSS grew out of Maharashtra, its initial Marathi colouring became irksome and a hindrance to expansion. In much of northern India, the ground for the RSS version of Hindu culture and organization had already been prepared by the Arya Samaj with its chain of educational centres (DAV and Gurukul Kangra) and identification of Hind-Hindi-Hindu. The 'Aryas', however, had begun as militant reformers. Dayanand's tradition of iconoclasm got much diluted over time, yet what had still survived in the 1930s was sufficient to breed a certain wariness about some of the aggressively idolatrous rituals and rites of the RSS. In deference to such sentiments Hedgewar abandoned the worship of Hanuman in RSS ritual, changed the language of prayer to Sanskrit, and generally toned

24

down insistence on rituals. Bajrangbali, of course, has come back today in a different context as organizations spawned by the RSS strive for a mass base much wider than the urban middle class. The impact of this change can be seen today in the house of the President, Lodi Road Arya Samaj, in Delhi, which prominently displays a huge icon of Bajrang Bali.

The Nagpur 'officers' training camp of 1940 was the last one to be attended by Hedgewar. Trainees came from all over the country, except from Assam, Orissa, and Kashmir. 'I see before my eyes today a miniature Hindu Rashtra,' declared Hedgewar in his last speech: words retold to us with much emotion by K.S. Sudarshan in course of his interview.

THE RSS UNDER GOLWALKAR IN THE FORTIES AND FIFTIES

In the interview he gave us in April 1991, K.S. Sudarshan's account of the RSS under Golwalkar revealed an interesting pattern of omissions and stresses. He said very little about the early Golwalkar years, but dilated at great length upon a speech of his in 1954 and subsequent developments. Sudarshan was talking to complete outsiders, at a time when the RSS and its affiliates want to project themselves as uniquely national. In the 1940s, the RSS had gone through a particularly aggressive phase, in theoretical formulation and activities alike: demonstratively aloof from the 1942 upsurge, violently active during the 1946–47 communal riots, suspected by many of complicity in the murder of Gandhi. Sudarshan's silence is understandable, but it cannot negate the abiding importance of this phase in RSS history. It remains a historical resource today for the RSS and its 'family', called upon to suit specific times and audiences (particularly, during riots). It is also exceptionally helpful for our understanding of precisely what the triumph of Hindutva will mean for our country.

In 1938, two years before he succeeded Hedgewar as *sarsangh-chalak*, M.S. Golwalkar published his *We or Our Nationhood Defined*, and later on many of his speeches and essays were published as *Bunch of Thoughts*. Golwalkar's theoretical writings clearly take V.D. Savarkar's *Hindutva* as their starting point (along with Baburao Savarkar's

Marathi treatise *Rashtra Mimansa*), but elaborate their ideas into a full-fledged conception of what he liked to call 'cultural nationalism' as distinct from 'territorial nationalism'. Hedgewar, too, had been acutely aware of this distinction. In the words of his biographer, 'In those days the idea of territorial nationalism held sway in the country. Even well-educated workers had developed a strong feeling that all those who live within the geographical boundaries of the country, whatever their sentiments, constitute the nation.'[14] Savarkar, we may recall, had kept a certain link with territorial nationalism through his concept of *pitribhumi*, but had then shifted his emphasis towards Hindu 'sentiments' or 'culture' by arguing that only among Hindus could *pitribhumi* and *punyabhumi* be identical. It was left to Golwalkar to bring out the implications, in all their totalitarian fullness.

We or Our Nationhood Defined explicitly models 'cultural nationalism' on Adolf Hitler:

> German national pride has now become the topic of the day. To keep up the purity of the nation and its culture, Germany shocked the world by her purging the country of the semitic races—the Jews. National pride at its highest has been manifested here. Germany has also shown how well-nigh impossible it is for races and cultures, having differences going to the root, to be assimilated into one united whole, a good lesson for us in Hindustan to learn and profit by.[15]

Golwalkar then proceeds to spell out the Indian implications of what he had learnt from Nazism with enviable clarity:

> From this standpoint sanctioned by the experience of shrewd old nations, the non-Hindu people in Hindustan must either adopt the Hindu culture and language, must learn to respect and revere Hindu religion, must entertain no idea but the glorification of the Hindu nation i.e. they must not only give up their attitude of intolerance and ingratitude towards this land and its age-long traditions, but must also cultivate the positive attitude of love and devotion instead; in one word, they must cease to be foreigners or may stay in the country wholly subordinated to the Hindu nation claiming nothing,

deserving no privileges, far less any preferential treatment, not even citizen's rights.[16]

The RSS and its affiliates have never repudiated this definition of Hindu Rashtra, though they have not always been so explicit about it as Golwalkar was in 1938. The absolute opposition to the ideal of composite nationalism as enshrined in the constitution of secular India is abundantly clear, for that grants equal rights irrespective of religious creed and protection to minority cultures.

Yet, in a paradox that is only apparent, since it underlies the whole history of twentieth century Hindutva, Golwalkar is always ready to talk in the same breath of catholicity and 'unity in diversity' as the special (and superior) characteristics of Hinduism, as contrasted to Islam, Christianity, or Communism. Everywhere, beneath the much trumpeted veneer of flexible heterogeneity, there lies a kernel of homogenizing rigidity, and in our subsequent chapter on the VHP we shall see how this is embodied today in two images of Ram. Here is Golwalkar again:

> ...this great country of ours extending in the north from the Himalayas—with all its branches spreading north, south, east and west, and with the territories included in those great branches—right up to the southern ocean inclusive of all the islands is one great natural unit. As the child of this soil, our well-evolved society has been living here for thousands of years. The society has been known, especially in modern times, as the Hindu society. This is also a historical fact. For it is the forefathers of the Hindu People who have set up standards and traditions...prescribed duties and rights...(and) shed their blood in defence of the sanctity and integrity of the Motherland. That all this has been done only by the Hindu People is a fact to which our history of thousands of years bears eloquent testimony. It means that only the Hindu has been living here as a child of this soil.[17]

As for Indian Muslims and Christians, 'They are born in this land, no doubt. But are they true to its salt?...*No.* Together with the change in their faith, gone are the spirit of love and devotion for the nation.'[18] The only test of patriotism, then, is to be allegiance to the so-called religion of the land.

All Muslims, in particular, are by definition traitors:

> They have also developed a feeling of identification with the enemies of this land. They look to some foreign lands as their holy places. They call themselves Sheikhs and Syeds...They still think they have come here to conquer and establish their kingdoms. So we see that it is not merely a case of change of faith, but a change even in national identity. What else is it if not treason, to join the camp of the enemy leaving the mother nation in the lurch?[19]

A glance through some issues of the *Organiser* is sufficient to indicate that Golwalkar's statements were not aberrations, but part of a coherent, continuous ideological tradition. Urdu is strongly condemned as a foreign language embodying subjugation, despite the fact that it was born in India. One article thunders: 'Let not another Pakistan be in the name of Urdu.'[20] Similarly, Indian Christians are condemned for allegedly preferring the English language, instead of Sanskrit or Hindi. Jainism and Buddhism also come in for denigration: 'they have never made any contribution to economic and philosophical thought as such...'[21] Against the much-touted propaganda today that the BJP-VHP-RSS, combine is only fighting 'pseudo-secularism' (and therefore, are presumably the only true secularists) we may counterpose the following passages from the *Organiser*:

> All that the Hindu wants is that our culture should flower forth into greatness. He is scandalized that after installing one Muslim as President and another Muslim as Chief Justice, he is told that he is not giving jobs to the Muslims...Muslims must accept the fact that India is as much a Hindu country as Pakistan is a Muslim country or Britain is a Christian country.[22]

While politicians may play with the words 'communal' and 'secular' to their hearts' content, the fact is that the predominant culture of a country will be its basic national culture.

Recalling the proverbial story of Mohammed going to the mountain, the article concludes:

> In the Indian situation, the Hindu is the mountain, and the Muslim population, Mohammed. I need not elaborate.[23]

After beginning on a note of sweet reasonableness and catholicity, and having carefully avoided references to the early Golwalkar, K.S. Sudarshan, too, launched on a violent harangue against Muslims towards the end of his interview. It may be recalled that B.L. Sharma of the VHP, a far more abrasive speaker, had a simpler approach: 'They have lust in their eyes,' he told us, 'and they breed too much.' He wove his entire discourse on the single theme—Muslim violence and lust.

Golwalkar developed his exclusivist logic to bring in one more target: socialist or communist ideas, which, too, could be branded as being of 'foreign' origin. But he was strangely reticent about the foreigners who were actually ruling the country when *We or Our Nationhood Defined* was published and his writings even include a passage that was critical of anti-British nationalism:

> The theories of territorial nationalism and of common danger, which formed the basis for our concept of nation, had deprived us of the positive and inspiring content of our real Hindu nationhood and made many of the freedom movements virtually anti-British movements. Being anti-British was equated with patriotism and nationalism. This reactionary view has had disastrous effects upon the entire course of the independence struggle, its leaders and the common people.[24]

The RSS therefore kept totally aloof from the many anti-British movements of the 1940s: the individual civil disobedience of 1940–41, the Quit India struggle, Azad Hind Fauj, the 1945–46 upsurges around the INA trials and the Bombay naval mutiny. Yet the early and mid-1940s remained a period of rapid growth, with the number of *shakhas* doubling between 1940 and '42, and with 10,000 *swayamsevaks* being trained by 1945 in Officers Training Camps (now set up in nearly every province), Like the Muslim League and the other Hindu communal groups, the RSS, too, benefited from the fact that it was never a target for British wartime repression. But much more important was the way in which Hindu and Muslim communalism were feeding into each other, with the drive for Pakistan making more and more Hindus feel that the RSS was their best and perhaps only defender. Such sentiments spread particularly among the Hindus of the Muslim-majority province of Punjab, as well as in UP where there was a highly articulate and aggressive Muslim leadership. A section of the Congress, too, had come to consider the RSS a useful bulwark against the increasing intransigence of the Muslim League. In Bengal, the other major Muslim-majority area, in contrast, the already-powerful progressive and Left traditions were able to block large-scale RSS inroads. Taking the country as a whole, however, recruits were trooping into *shakhas*, and money, too, was pouring in. It was a time of prosperity for trading groups, with ample opportunities for war contracts and profiteering, and traders have always provided the major social bases for the RSS. Significant inroads seem to have been made during these years into government services also.

The communal holocaust of 1946–47, ushered in by Jinnah's call for Direct Action and the Great Calcutta Killings of August 1946, was regarded as its 'finest hour' by the RSS. Through active participation in riots, relief work in Hindu refugee camps and virulent communal propaganda, the RSS contributed vastly to the development of a massive fear psychosis among large sections of Hindus about the 'foreign' Muslims. Even a section of the Congress High Command, particularly Vallabhbhai Patel, had become fairly sympathetic towards the RSS, although Nehru remained bitterly hostile. In the interviews they gave us, K.S. Sudarshan kept discreetly quiet about these bloodstained years; B.L. Sharma, however, boasted openly about his active role in the Punjab riots.

The onward march of the RSS was abruptly halted by the impact of the murder of Mahatma Gandhi. Nathuram Godse had left the organization many years back, but no one could deny that he had been initially trained by it, and RSS rhetoric about 'appeasement' of Muslims seemed all but indistinguishable from the justifications offered for the assassination. Golwalkar sent telegrams expressing shock to Nehru and Patel, and *shakha* work was suspended for 13 days 'out of respect' for 'Mahatmaji'. But popular suspicion and anger could not be allayed so easily. RSS offices and houses of its members were attacked in many parts of the country, particularly in Maharashtra where popular anger took an anti-Brahmin turn. On 4 February 1948, the Government of India declared the RSS illegal.

The *shakhas* lay low, confining themselves to 'social functions' and quiet group discussions. The organization in fact crumbled quite rapidly, despite its much-vaunted discipline and militancy, even though repression was never very severe—much less so than what the Communists were facing in the same period. The main response was to approach eminent personalities in efforts to persuade the Government to lift the ban. In August 1948 Golwalkar began a correspondence with that goal with Nehru and Patel. His letters to both on 24 September 1948 harp on the alleged danger from Communism, as evidenced by 'the alarming happenings in Burma, Indochina, Java and other neighboring states'. The Indian youth were strongly attracted, for 'the one effective check of the RSS no longer exists'. The RSS, he pleaded with Nehru, should therefore be allowed 'to work honourably and help the government fight the menace—on its own cultural lines'. He assured Patel that 'if you with government power and we with organized cultural force combine, we can soon eliminate this menace.'[25] As could have been expected, Nehru remained unimpressed, and even the more sympathetic Patel wanted proof that the RSS was ready to change its ways. Other methods to get the ban removed proved equally abortive: a signature campaign, which could rope in only 9 lakhs, a Jana Adhikar Samiti chaired by Acharya Kripalani, and finally, in December 1948, a brief *satyagraha*, in which some 60,000 *swayamsevaks* courted arrest. Golwalkar called off the *satyagraha* in January 1949, and resumed negotiations in which interestingly, G.D. Birla acted as one of the mediators. Eventually the RSS agreed to adopt a written constitution, maintain regular registers of members, not to admit minors without parental permission, and work openly and in the cultural field only. The RSS won back its legality on 12 July 1949 in this way, agreeing to conditions which were general enough not to seriously hamper its work, but which still represented a humiliating surrender under pressure. The contrast with Communist behaviour in the same years is rather illuminating. The RSS leader wrote letters from jail offering cooperation: Communists opened 'jail fronts' to carry on militant confrontations even inside prisons.

The decade that followed lifting of the ban was not, on the whole, a happy one for the RSS or other right-wing groups. Communists emerged as the principal opposition to the Congress in the 1952 elections, and made further gains in 1957, forming a government in Kerala. For Centrist forces, these were the golden years of Nehruvian 'socialism' and successful non-alignment, of a certain move to the Left, which, then as well as later on, has tended to marginalise right-wing forces. The RSS itself in the early 1950s was plagued by internal disunion; the *pracharaks* (full-time cadres) had perforce functioned largely on their own under conditions of illegality, and it took some time for the central leadership to re-assert its full control. K.S. Sudarshan recalled also a certain sense of ideological vacuum, a confusion about RSS aims in the new situation of independence, parliamentary democracy, and a secular constitution. As often in RSS history, internal tensions tended to take the form of a 'culture'/'politics' conflict. The older generation on the whole wanted to persist in quiet organizational-cultural work; many younger members demanded more activist postures and interventions.

Golwalkar revealed his qualities of leadership in the two major initiatives—ideological and organizational—which he and his associates took in confronting this near crisis of the early 1950s. In March 1954, he refurbished the ideological arsenal of the RSS through a long speech at a conference of district organizers which K.S. Sudarshan recalled for us in great detail. In the self-image of the RSS today, it appears, this speech constitutes the 'philosophical' foundation of a Hindutva brought up-to-date to suit contemporary conditions. This is a 'positive' Hinduism, based on *angangibhava* ('limb-body' relations—roughly, organicity). A hierarchy is postulated of individual-society/family-nature-divinity (*vyakti-samaj/parivar-prakriti-paramatma*), and men can reach God only through reverence for society and nature. Society is immediately identified with familiar relations, which would evidently provide the paternalist model for all other relationships, including that between ruler and ruled. Contrary to Western ideals, we are told, this is a philosophy which gives precedence to duty towards the community over individualism and materialism. Western individualism shatters family and community, Hinduism integrates them through a harmonious *dharma*—which, Sudarshan explained, rests on the right balance between four *shaktis*: intelligence, power, wealth and labour (*buddhi/raj/dhana/srama*).

The discourse has the great advantage of pointing in several directions at the same time. The four-fold distinction-cum-harmony of *shaktis* would satisfy traditional admirers of *varnasrama*, for it is no more than a restatement of the old Brahmanical doctrine, with the *srama* associated with the Shudra, who is placed, as always, at the bottom. At the same time, Sudarshan's exposition made clear to us how conveniently open the doctrine is to certain very fashionable tendencies in contemporary Western intellectual discourses. Sudarshan spent some time trying to convince us that true Hinduism is based on *sristhi-dharma*, which is nothing but ecology. The individual and society must seek a proper balance with *prakriti*, and the age-old Hindu veneration for the Ganga and the cow are rationalized as remarkable anticipations of modern ecological ideals. The RSS, however, has so far displayed no active concern or interest about the ecological movements going on within the country. The BJP Government's stand in Madhya Pradesh over the Narmada Valley Project would constitute a particularly telling example of the gap between its self-image and practice. Interestingly, religion is, after all, made ultimately acceptable through the sanction of science. What *angangibhava* deliberately occludes is of course the theme of exploitation, whether of class, caste, or gender: the familial model is thought sufficient for ideal harmony, as if the family itself cannot be a site for tension or oppression.

Much more important was the organizational initiative to set up a series of affiliates or 'family' members. The RSS itself would concentrate as before upon unostentatious cadre-training and 'culture', thus keeping to the letter of the 1949 agreement with the Government; many of its important cadres, however, would be sent out to found and to work in organizations catering to specific social groups and/or with specialized aims, including electoral politics. Cohesion and stability could then be combined with widening spread and great flexibility. It could, through an electoral front, seek direct political power, and yet, by continuing its regular *shakha* activity, maintain a reputation for disinterested, cultural, character-building concerns.

With the emergence of the RSS affiliates, Hindutva entered a new and more dynamic period of its history, culminating in the present strength of the RSS-VHP-BJP combine. A closer look at RSS organizations and the structure of its relations with its 'family' seems indispensable at this point.

ORGANIZATIONAL STRUCTURE OF THE RSS FAMILY

The one-word answer that a *swayamsevak* will give if asked about the aims of the RSS is *sangathan*. Organization, in fact, has primacy over theoretical programmes or specific policies, and, from its inception at Nagpur in 1925–26 till today, the *shakha* has been the basic organizational cell of the RSS: reproduced in identical form in every part of the country and the key to all its work.

Many RSS publications include a vivid description by Golwalkar of daily life in a *shakha*. Young men and boys, he tells us, begin with '*Bharatiya* games' in an 'open playground under a saffron flag'. Then 'the leader's whistle or order has a magical effect on them: there is instant perfect order and silence.' There is next a round of physical exercises—'*lathi, suryanamaskar*, marching, etc.', followed by collective singing of a patriotic song. 'Discussions follow. They delve deep into the problems affecting the national life. And finally they stand in a row before the flag and recite the prayer: Many salutations to thee, O loving motherland!' The proceedings end with '*Bharat mata ki jai*'.[26]

What is interesting here is the juxtaposition and balancing of opposites: boys romping around, playing in an 'open playground', who stiffen into martial stances at the 'whistle or call from their leaders'; the ability to wield both play on the one hand and authority and discipline on the other; the paramilitary formation that invisibly exists beyond the playground. Physical training in the RSS is only the means to the end of a psychological drill leading to a total surrender of individuality to what the RSS likes to call the 'ideal'. Very relevant in this context is a story Golwalkar loved to relate, of a rich man who, seeing a beautiful peacock in his garden one day, gave it some opium mixed with food. The peacock started coming every day, and eventually got 'so habituated that it used to come regularly at that hour, even without that opium'. Implicit in the parable, of course, is the sense of trapping the game through a bait that leads on to something very different. Golwalkar identified 'three factors' in this technique of habit formation: 'constant meditation of ideal that is to be formed into a *samskar*': 'constant company of persons devoted to the same ideal'; and 'engaging the body in activities congenial to that ideal'.[27] *Shakhas*, therefore, orient the body, the mind and the immediate environment entirely and on identical lines.

It is not surprising, given this basic approach, that Hedgewar began with boys of 12 to 15, and that the RSS has always tried to catch its recruits at a very tender and impressionable age. Its totalitarianism is therefore significantly different from the classic fascist model which moulded cadres from a higher age-level. 'Leave aside the minds already crammed with well-formed opinions,' RSS workers are told, 'and concentrate on clean slates.' Since the organization has primarily pedagogical functions—to train cadres for wider fronts—it seeks to monopolize the sources of pedagogy by starting with clean slates. On these the political message gets inscribed through oral exposition of a few fairly simple basic themes in a face-to-face situation where the *pracharak* gives and the disciples receive; an entirely non-dialogic, non-argumentative mode of learning which leaves, as we saw through our own questions, teachers quite unequipped to deal with questioning.

The games-cum-physical culture aspect of *shakhas* have a major appeal, particularly in the overcrowded lower middle class living areas in the city or small-town neighbourhoods, where alternative recreational facilities may well be absent. As training proceeds, RSS recruits acquire a new sense of corporate identity. This is often desperately desired among traders, shopkeepers, clerks, and petty professionals—men with lives otherwise bitterly competitive and separated, who feel demoralized and lost in a still partly unfamiliar and rapidly changing environment. The successful among them might well feel even more isolated and fragmented, and, as with Hindu trading communities in north Indian towns in the past,[28] investment in modern forms of the sacred perhaps becomes the principal mode of assuaging a sense of guilt over individual profit as well as an anchorage in traditional collectivist moorings which do not threaten class interest. Such appeals are likely to be all the greater under conditions of rapid urbanization and small-town growth, characteristic of many parts of the country today. A group and a god are necessary here, and the RSS provides both. It is significant that RSS *shakhas* have always had much less appeal in villages, with open spaces and a more rooted sense of community. In villages too, the community is experienced as a series of oppositions and exclusions as well as some kind of mutual link. In towns and cities, life can be lived much more entirely within one's own class and caste without constant physical contacts with different groups. In a sense, then, the image of a unified Hindu community may go less challenged within an urban situation.

RSS identity is exclusivist, based on a self-image of moral and physical superiority—but at the same time it is conveniently free of dangers of non-conformity or rebellion. The RSS teaches its youth to revere elders, and entry into it normally does not involve familial conflict. The fairly brief *shakha* routine does not disrupt studies, and, with the deepening penetration of the ideology of Hindutva to which the RSS itself has contributed so much, the basic ideals would have become the common sense of many relatives, friends and neighbours. Our case study of Khurja gave us an almost claustrophobic sense of a small-town Hindu trade-cum-professional milieu where any alternative culture seems, quite simply, non-existent: the young men move from communal-minded families to schools and colleges full of RSS teachers, and RSS *shakhas* provide, practically the only other source of recreation, leisure-time socialization, and intellectual training.

What adds to the RSS appeal is the basic simplicity of its ideological message, preached in a style that deliberately avoids complexities and debates, and inculcated simultaneously via a whole battery of rituals and symbols. No major intellectual effort, or mastering of difficult texts, is required—unlike, say, in Marxism. RSS bookshops are bare of serious or substantive publications. Cadres are not meant to read closely and reflect, through developing stages of understanding, on a few crucial texts like the *Gita* or the *Ramayana* which do not have the same significance or function as they had in different phases of the national and revolutionary movements. The contrast with the theoretical reflection within any branch of Marxism could not be greater. By linking up with the uses of the audio-visual media by the VHP at a later stage, it seems to have bypassed the literate stage altogether. The core doctrine can be summed up in a handful of propositions. Hindu, and Hindus alone, constitute the Indian nation, since they are the original inhabitants and sole creators of its society and culture. Hinduism is uniquely catholic and tolerant, and hence superior to any other faith, but its tolerance has often been mistaken for weakness. The Hindu nation has been repeatedly conquered by aliens, particularly Muslims and then the Christian British, and must acquire strength through RSS *sangathan* to counter all present and future threats. The subsequent entry and takeover by foreigners created the illusion that India was a land of many different and equal cultures. In truth, however, all cultural traditions survived by Hinduizing themselves—otherwise they remained alien, distanced, oppressive. It was the Western form of knowledge, proceeding through classificatory and divisive modes of perception, that systematized and popularized the idea that India lacked a homogeneous civilization and a single community. 'Pseudo-secular' nationalists like Nehru, who preferred the bondage to an alien system of thought, perpetuated it by integrating this notion within the 'pseudo-secular' constitution. This must be changed and only a 'truly secular' Hindu Rashtra will afford protection to non-Hindus. The threats remain, because the present state is ruled by traitors to the Hindu nation, 'pseudo-secularists' who 'appeased' Muslims in their pursuit of a politics of 'vote banks'.

The glaring flaws here would be fairly obvious: most notably, the unproved assumption that 'Hindus' are, and have always consti-tuted, a fundamentally homogeneous and unchanging bloc. The charge of 'Muslim appeasement' is equally absurd, for the minority community is grossly unrepresented in every kind of contemporary elite (whether administrative, police, military, business, academic or professional) and Muslims have comprised the vast majority of riot victims in post-Independence communal clashes (most notably from the early 1980s onwards). RSS recruits, however, are disciplined from boyhood onwards to ignore argument, and a discourse of Hindu harmony that glosses over tensions of class, caste and gender fits in well with the presuppositions of an entirely male and pre-dominantly high caste, middle and lower middle class membership.

Formal intellectual training in the *shakhas* takes place at least once a week through *bauddhik* classes conducted by full-time cadres (*pracharaks*). The lectures are enlivened by illustrations from mythology and RSS-tailored history, but can also include simple catechisms of brief questions and answers. They deliberately avoid conceptual subtleties, and represent a straightforward rhetorical assault on the emotions. Our interview with K.S. Sudarshan gave us a taste of the mode of discoursing, for we were talking to a full-time cadre of many years' standing. We had come without any prior notice, yet Sudarshan was able to immediately launch out into an unhurried, good-humoured, coherent, fairly systematic exposition lasting over three hours. Except towards the end when he suddenly launched an anti-Muslim tirade, the style was. quiet and relaxed, expository rather than exhortatory, with many parables and even one or two risqué jokes. There was a striking absence of reference to any basic text. RSS learning practice seems to rely heavily on morality alone, maintaining a total control that might have been difficult to ensure if recruits had been encouraged to read widely by themselves. The high-ranking RSS leader knew he was talking to a group of University teachers, but the level of exposition remained commonsensical, and never went into subtleties of Hindu philosophy or religion. Evidently in the *shakha* the *pracharak* talks, the members listen, learn and revere. As K.S. Malkani puts it, *shakha* training produces 'certitudes'—the RSS does not encourage 'doubting Thomases'.[29]

Unquestioning, disciplined faith is inculcated above all through evocative symbols and rituals. The saffron flag flies over the *shakha* playground, and a favourite RSS game ends with the cry: '*Hindustan Hindu ka, nahi kisi ke baap ka*'. Golwalkar emphasized this ritual dimension by drawing an explicit parallel with Hindu sects:

> Without a suitable technique no ideal, however great, can be realized...A Shaiva, a Shakta, or a Vaishnava, each has his own method of worship, his own ritual, his codes and connections regulating his own life. We too have evolved a technique, an emblem, a *mantra* and a code of discipline in keeping with our ideal of an unified and disciplined national life.[30]

There are a few Sanskrit mantras with which all *sevaks* are meant to begin the day, begin their meals, and which they chant before sleep.

The day is closed with a singing of the entire hymn of *Bande Mataram* by Bankim Chandra, its Bengali parts included. The entirety is given special emphasis since the hymn supposedly encompasses the authentic shape of undivided pre-partition *Bharatmata*: an abbreviation of the hymn, consequently, implies a symbolic surrender of her symbolic integrity. As the saffron flag rather than the tricolour is regarded as the true national flag, this hymn is similarly affirmed to be the true national hymn. Rabindranath's *'Jana gana mana'* is expunged, by expounding the false myth that the poet had composed it not to salute the country but to greet George V.

The fundamental tenet for the RSS is Hindu *sangathan*, the emblem is the *bhagwa dhwaj* (worshipped as *guru*), the khaki shorts uniform (remarkably non-indigenous, by the way, and copied from the British Indian police and army) and *lathi* serve as the distinctive dress, the daily *shakhas* with their rituals constitute the core of discipline. And, like all religious sects, the RSS has its festivals, which are six in number: *Navaratri-Vijaya Dashami*, celebrating Ram's victory over Ravana, when weapons are worshipped and *shakhas* take out route marches; *Makarsankranti* in January, to foster 'integral nationalism', *Varsh-pratipada* in April, when Yudhishthir and Vikramaditya supposedly started the old Hindu calendar year and Ram was crowned; *Hindu Samrajya Diwas* in May, to celebrate the coronation of Shivaji; *Rakshabandhan* in August, to remind *swayamsevaks* of the duty to sacrifice life itself, if needed, and to protect the honour of Hindu society; and *Vyas Puja* in September, when the *bhagwa dhwaj* is worshipped and members make anonymous donations to the organization. These donations incidentally constitute the basic funds of the RSS. No records or receipts are apparently maintained, enabling a unique flexibility, secretiveness, and leadership control in matters of finance.

Four out of the six RSS festivals are appropriated from the traditional Hindu calendar. All have been given a highly martial colour and a 'national' reinterpretation. Significantly, however, there is no festival derived from the history of the modern, anti-British national movement: not even 1857, which Savarkar had once hailed as the first national war of independence. The appropriation of traditional Hindu rituals for a moral *rashtriya* objective is also a two-way process. As we shall see in a later section, the RSS from the early 1980s has deliberately moved the location of some of their festivals, originally held within *shakha* confines, into temples, making them occasions for propaganda work among temple devotees and visitors. The interpenetration of *dharmik* and *rashtriya*, religious and 'national', is geared towards modifying the meanings of both. If Hinduism is 'nationalized', the nation is to be in the same measure Hinduized. The basic logic of Savarkar is still very much at work; B.L. Sharma, for instance, insisted that not only Ram, but Hanuman, has to be revered by everyone as 'the commander-in-chief of the Hindu nation'.

The steel frame that welds the multitude of *shakhas* into a monolithic whole is apexed by the *sarsanghchalak* (nominated by his predecessor on a life-time basis), *sarkaryavahak* (general secretary) and *prachar pramukh* (chief organizer) and manned basically by *pracharaks* (a term borrowed from Hindu sects that have gone in for proselytizing). All these are full-time cadres, and are usually expected to remain unmarried. The distractions of married life and parenthood are thus avoided, and the RSS full-time cadres, through their celibate way of life, acquire an element of ascetic sacredness without being *sanyasis* themselves. A Vishwa Hindu Parishad leader in his interview with us explained in these terms Golwalkar's success in building bridges with the world of *sants* and *sadhus* while floating the VHP from 1960.[31]

The *sarsanghchalak* gives an annual address laying down the tasks of the coming year, and this is conveyed down the chain of command in more or less the same style to the *shakhas*. The basically undemocratic structure of the RSS is indicated by a marked discrepancy between organizational theory and practice. The written constitution of 1949, a concession to governmental pressure, gave a lot of power to local and provincial level *sanghchalaks*, and made them elective. But elections have remained largely formal and, despite the similarity in title between *sarsanghchalak* and *sanghchalak*, the latter is often a decorative post. *Sanghchalaks* do not have to be full-time workers, and it is the *pracharak*, appointed and controlled strictly from the top, who is the real kingpin of the whole organization. The 'Officers Training Camps' are basically for *pracharaks* and the latter have also been the instrument for setting up and managing the growing family of RSS affiliates.

The inner life of the RSS seems to be a blend of iron discipline and a certain human touch, to which the 'family' ideology no doubt contributes. 'We go to *shakhas*, we visit people's homes, we look after people's problems. If a person is ill, we ask if he has money. If this answer is negative, we borrow from others to lend him some.' Such was the account of RSS life given to a member of our group by Chakrabarti Radhey Lal Awasthi, an ex-*pracharak*, now a trader in Tisthi village near Bilhaur (Central U.P.). But it is the discipline that remains the most striking—and formidable—dimension of the RSS. Thus a regular question put to *shakha* recruits is: 'What will you do if your officer (*adhikari*) asks you to jump into a well?' The expected answer is 'I will do so immediately,' and those who hesitate are mercilessly jeered at. The combination of martial discipline and familial ideology has managed—so far—to keep together a bewildering number of affiliates of apparently very diverse character.

The RSS is virtually unique among modern Indian socio-political organizations in being exclusively male. It did, however, set up a women's branch, the Rashtrasevika Samiti, the first, in fact, of its affiliates, way back in 1936. The *Rashtrasevikas* have kept a rather low profile, and Sudarshan even forgot to mention them in an otherwise comprehensive account of RSS affiliates. Growth has been slow, with about one lakh members now—as compared, say, to 29 lakhs in the All India Democratic Women's Association (AIDWA) linked to the CPI(M), and founded only in 1981. Even in Delhi, where the Left is extremely weak, the Janwadi Mahila Samiti affiliated to the AIDWA has 15,000 members and significant bases in labouring areas: the 2000 members of the Rashtrasevika Samiti are confined almost entirely to middle class neighbourhoods. In sharp and significant contrast to most Left and feminist groups, the *Rashtrasevikas* have preferred to work in a more or less same-class situation.

The internal structure of the Rashtrasevika Samiti is closely modeled on the RSS, with a *pramukh sanghchalak* nominating her successor, unmarried *pracharikas* as full-time cadres, daily *shakhas* providing physical-cum-intellectual training, and all the RSS festivals except the *Shivaji Utsav* being observed. A *dharmapatni* model, related but subordinate to the male body, seems to be at work: members are not *swayamsevikas* but more modestly entitled *rashtrasevikas*, and everyone we met had relatives in the RSS. There is also

41

a greater stress on family work outside *shakhas*. Simple daily rituals are prescribed for home use, with even a 'correspondence course' of postal instructions for those who, after marriage, are unable to attend the *shakhas*. Members make it a point to visit each other's homes, help out in domestic crises, and maintain contact even with those who can no longer find time for Samiti work. Ideology is spread through sustained kinship and neighbourhood contact with non-*Rashtrasevika* women, and there is a system of informal training for unaffiliated wives of RSS members and sympathizers. Educational work is carried on through the closely related Saraswati Shishu Mandir network, but otherwise there is little emphasis on charity or social welfare, or, of course, on militant mobilization around gender or class issues. Golwalkar's instructions for women had carved out a sort of a *'Lakshmangandi'* of faithful motherhood in which the women affiliated to the RSS would confine themselves to the proper training of children and spreading the word through quiet domestic and neighbourhood contacts with her sisters. Members pool resources to reduce the burden of dowry, instead of campaigning against it. *Sevikas* are always told to try persuasion, but never openly revolt against their families, in matters of choice of husband, marital ill-treatment, or even participation in Samiti work. The Samiti differs from other women's organizations, as a member told us, *hum ghar torne wali nahin hain* (we are not wreckers of homes). They disapprove of divorce and offer no legal counselling to women fighting against their families for their rights. Theoretically there are no caste restrictions on membership, but caste—like class and gender—is never discussed in a contentious way in *bauddhik* sessions.

Yet, to dismiss the *Rashtrasevikas* as relatively unimportant and hamstrung by a monolithic patriarchal ideology, would be a serious mistake: the massive turnout of *kar sevikas* at Ayodhya, often trained and sent by the Samiti, provides a sufficient warning against any such underestimation. The same-class situation in which the Samiti has operated facilitates easy, informal interaction, a surprising self-confidence and articulation even among junior members in the presence of their seniors. The Samiti, like the RSS as a whole, has pursued a strategy of slow, socially limited, but extremely intensive mobilization: a family-to-family, mind-to-mind percolation of Hin-

dutva, almost, one might say, a Gramscian construction of hegemony on a molecular model. The *bauddhik* programme in *shakhas*,
along with informal discussions in homes, meets a very real hunger
for serious, yet easily comprehensible, intellectual discussion among
women with lives otherwise largely bereft of such mental food. Pa-
tient sustained work across several generation underlie the recent,
apparently sudden and deceptively spontaneous entry of women
from very conservative backgrounds into public spaces in an aggressively communal cause, epitomized by the prominence of Sadhvi
Rithambara and Uma Bharati.

Nor is the ideology conservatively patriarchal in an unqualified
sense: there may be a potential for certain tensions, even ruptures.
The decision to participate in public, confrontationist *kar seva*, a
Rashtrasevika told our interviewer, had been opposed by the elders,
but pushed through by young militants. A *Rashtrasevika* violently
condemned *sati*, and ruled out any possibility of its ever being vol-
untary: evidently, as with post-1920s Hindutva in general, a simple
model of 'fundamentalist revival' will not work. The Samiti journal
Jagriti glorifies ancient Hindu womanhood in the conventionally
revivalist manner, but also occasionally carries fairly sympathetic
accounts of contemporary women's movements. One article argues
the need for the economic independence of women, and even demands reservations in employment of women judges. Even the
training programme, geared to produce powerful self-confident bodies, might perhaps acquire unintended meanings in a context
marked by male harassment, typical of the north Indian urban middle class environment where the Samiti has its bases. Perhaps the
implicit conflict finds expression also in two slightly different origin
myths of the Samiti. The RSS account is that Hedgewar was ap-
proached by Mrs. Kelkar with a request to permit women to enter
the organization; 'Doctorji' persuaded her to start the Rashtrasevika
Samiti instead. The official Samiti history underplays Hedgewar's
role, and a *Rashtrasevika* told us that Mrs. Kelkar had been con-
vinced of the need for such an organization after witnessing a Hindu
girl being raped on a train by *goondas* in the presence of her pusil-
lanimous husband—and the *goondas*, interestingly, were not
Muslims but Hindus.

The *Jagriti* cover depicts two helpless, crouching women against a dark background, out of which steps out a young, rather grim-faced woman, with firm steps, uplifted head, tightly-draped sari, no traditional Hindu marks of *sindur*, veil, or *bindi*—but wearing the Samiti uniform of white sari with purple border. The image indicates the paradox of the *Rashtrasevikas*—undoubtedly empowering in some ways, but bringing women from a traditionally conservative social stratum into public space in a regimented, colourless, grim manner, in a violent campaign of blind hatred geared to produce citizens of an authoritarian Hindu Rashtra, on the ruins of secular, democratic politics. Whether Hindutva would be able to sustain this paradox, so far a source of strength, remains an open question—though it would be dangerous to underestimate the formidable suppleness of its ideology.[32]

Sudarshan claimed the Bharatiya Mazdur Sangh (BMS)—actually set up in 1955—as the first, chronologically, of the RSS affiliates, and explicitly related its foundation to the urgent need to counter the influence of Communist class-war ideas ('haves and have-nots') among workers. Rejecting class struggle, the BMS claims to be critical also of the capitalist greed for profit. Echoing a favourite theme of Golwalkar's *Bunch of Thoughts*, and at times appropriating some Gandhian ideas, the BMS rejects both capitalism and communism as Western materialist notions, and puts forward as the Indian or Hindu alternative the ideal of converting enterprises into occupational 'families'. Workers should be invited to participate in management, and in return must cultivate harmonious relations with their employers: strikes are permitted only as a last resort, after conciliation efforts have failed. The BMS motto is 'labourize industry, industrialize the nation, nationalize labour'. The total rejection of ideas of international labour solidarity is embodied in the effort to replace May Day by *Viswakarma Puja*. Few efforts seem to have been made, however, to implement such long-term (and vague) ideals, and the BMS in practice probably operates as a fairly conventional, if milder than usual, trade union. Specific labour participation under the BMS banner in the recent RSS-VHP-BJP movements has not been very prominent—though a group of Bhilai workers at the VHP Delhi rally of 4 April 1991 did tell us that some BMS units had sent volunteers for the Ayodhya *kar seva*.

If the labour front of the RSS, though numerically far from neggible, has remained somewhat marginal to its principal concerns, access or even efforts, in mobilizing peasants or agricultural labourers have been almost conspicuous by their absence. Both the ayat Sangh of 1971 and the Kisan Sangh of 1979 remained shadowy organizations. The main thrust has always been among educated middle class groups, and so it is not surprising that the Akhil haratiya Vidyarthi Parishad (ABVP) was floated way back in 1948. he ideal of this student affiliate of the RSS is to restructure relations between teachers, students and college managements on the mily model, and administrators and teachers can also become its members. The Vidyarthi Parishad has a *Vyas Puja* where students ay homage to teachers. As with the BMS, however, the actual anctioning of the ABVP within student politics (contesting elections, running unions, occasional agitation on student demands, tc.) has not been markedly differently from that of organizations ffiliated to other political tendencies. Its main utility has probably onsisted in recruiting RSS cadres from the college student community.

Much more distinctive is the sustained effort of the RSS to penetrate the world of schools. Education has been absolutely central o the entire RSS enterprise: a *Rashtrasevika* told us that her organization is geared to 'class' (in the sense of teaching), as distinct om 'mass' work. The first Shishu Mandir (a significant title) was et up at Gorakhpur in the 1950s and now, Sudarshan claimed, 000 such institutions are functioning under the Vidya Bharati cheme, going up to high school and occasionally college level. The ʹidya Bharati was set up in 1977 to coordinate school activities. While Shishu Mandirs teach primary school children, Bal Mandirs each at High School level and Samskar Kendras, or informal schooling is provided for urban slums, forest areas or remote villages. hishu and Bal Mandirs exist for the middle classes and charge fairly igh fees—Rs 175 for Bal Mandirs and Rs 100 for Shishu Mandirs n Delhi. Dr. Meenakshi Sharma, Principal, Bal Mandir at Jhandevalan, told us proudly that students come from 'good' families— actory owners, businessmen, doctors, teachers. She herself belongs o an RSS family and the bulk of the teachers are recruited from mong known people. For the teachers coming from outside the nown circle, strict supervision and training is continuously

maintained through regular teacher-training camps. Although th
Government prescribed syllabus is followed, frequent lectures on th
necessity of dying for one's religion, assembly and mealtime prayer
on the same theme, patriotic and devotional music and an overpow
ering visual display of the armed Ram, the future Ayodhya Temple
and of Hindu figures fighting Muslims, ensure the projection of
different and stronger message. The most important departure i
made through the annual test in 'Indian culture' for which each clas
is given a separate textbook. Written in a question-answer cate
chism format, this compendium enumerates lists of Hindu heroes—
especially those who fought Muslims—Hindu mythological figure
names of sacred texts, geographical spots and events, short comic
on messages of *Ramayana* and *Gita*. No Muslim or Christian name
intrude on this account on 'Indian culture'. The Vidya Bharati i
now reorganizing school syllabi in the four BJP run states.

They follow the usual courses after Class VIII, but include extr
lessons on Sanskrit, moral education, yoga, and 'national orienta
tion'. Shishu, Bal, and Balika Mandirs are most numerous, as coul
have been expected, in UP, MP, Delhi, Haryana and Rajasthan, bu
they are now also spreading into provinces like Andhra Pradesh. Th
broad RSS influence on education, it needs to be added, goes muc
beyond the range of schools directly controlled by it. A member o
our team found a Shishu Mandir and an adjoining DAV schoo
under the Arya Samaj remarkably similar in appearance and tone
In both, the usual colourful pictures and decorations one expects t
find in nursery schools were absent: birds, animals or flowers hav
been totally displaced by portraits of the standard Hindu-nationalis
pantheon. RSS ideological presence is also obvious in the world o
children's books. Unlike some other Indian languages, Hindi seem
to lack a developed genre of secular children's literature, and thi
has contributed to the spectacular success of the *Amar Chitra Kath*
series, which are prominently displayed in the RSS bookshop, Suru
chibhandarr, adjoining the organization's Delhi headquarters o
Keshab Kunj (Jhandewalla). Not unexpectedly, Sudarshan spen
some time describing RSS efforts to fight 'distortions' in history
among which he mentioned the view that Aryans had come as in
vaders, and the late dating of the epics. The RSS, we were told, i
working on a multi-volume comprehensive history of India.

The centrality of history-writing within the pedagogy of the Hindu Right is a long and continuous tradition. The Kangri Gurukul, in the first decade of the century, produced textbooks in Hindi to rewrite the history of India. The VHP today flourishes the arguments and counter arguments offered by sympathetic professional archaeologists to stake its claim over the Babri Mosque.

The early RSS had been imbued with a certain distrust of conventional politics, and the break with the Hindu Mahasabha under Golwalkar must have sharpened this 'culture'/'politics' divide. The device of setting up affiliate 'family' members provided a convenient way out of what had become a recurrent internal debate, and in 1931 Golwalkar sent RSS cadres to help Shyamaprasad Mukherjee, ex-Mahasabha leader (who had quit Nehru's Cabinet for its alleged appeasement of Pakistan), to start the Bharatiya Jan Sangh (BJS). The RSS thus came to have a frankly political extension, open to a considerable measure of pragmatism and flexibility—while retaining for itself the advantage of a claim to be purer and 'above' politics.

The BJP today, acknowledged successor to the BJS, is a mass party with formidable (and, in recent years, rapidly growing) electoral support, which yet embodies the paradox of being constituted by something like an absence: its cadres and ideology are overwhelmingly borrowed from a formally distinct organization, the RSS. The book shop attached to the BJP central office in New Delhi is strangely bare of ideological literature, and stocks little more than party conference reports and manifestos. It seems to generate no autonomous political doctrine and few cultural signs of its own particular existence beyond the high investment area of election propaganda: for which, of course, a wide variety of devices are deployed from wall slogans and photographs, to couplets and posters, stickers, *video raths*, rallies and motorcades. Since the *rath yatra* days of Advani, however, even the election campaign has become inextricably bound up with VHP activities. Advani's *rath* used and augmented VHP symbols and the movement, while the 4 April VHP rally at Delhi and the *Sant Sammelan* that preceded it were really the opening of the BJP's election campaign.

In his interview with us, Sunder Singh Bhandari, BJP Vice-President, began with a neat tripartite disjunction. The BJP, he said, is

47

'political', the VHP 'social', and the RSS 'organizational', and eac
is 'independent' in its own domain. The distinction quickly brol
down as he went on to add that all three were 'nationalist', and a
were guided by a 'culture', which was promptly equated with 'tl
Hindu ethos'. Bhandari, we learnt, has been in the RSS since 193
and belongs to the original batch of cadres (along with Deen Day
Upadhyay, Vajpayee, and Advani) sent by Golwalkar in 1951 (
start the BJS.

In 1965, Deen Dayal Upadhyay tried to give the Jan Sangh a
ostensibly distinct ideology and impart a veneer of flexibility an
openness to the Savarkar-Golwalkar framework through a series (
lectures to party members on 'integral humanism'. Upadhya
claimed to be 'scientific', welcomed Western science (as distinc
from Western 'ways of life'), and declared that even the principle
of *dharma* may have 'to be adapted to changing times and places
Certain economic objectives—like full employment and free educa
tion and medical treatment—were mentioned for the first time
without specifying concrete methods for realizing such laudabl
goals. There was little use of the word 'Hindu', and no obviou
abuse of Muslims.

The fundamentals, however, clearly remained unchanged. A re
erence was slipped in to the 'thousand-year-old struggle for free
dom', and Golwalkar quoted to the effect that while there are goo
and bad individuals among Hindus and Muslims alike, Hindus ar
distinctive in the way they 'always think of good things' whe
acting as a group. Change has to be in conformity with 'our cultur
that is our very nature', and here '*Bharatiya*' integral humanism i
opposed to both capitalist individualism and Marxist socialism, fo
these are based on the harmful Western idea that progress come
through conflict. The ideal, in contrast, is one of harmonious rela
tionships everywhere, as between a body and its limbs, applied t
man and nature, individual and society, labour and capital: an ob
vious echo of Golwalkar's *angangibhava*. In an interesting gloss or
Savarkar, the 'underlying unity' of '*bharatiya* culture' is located, no
so much in a place of origin as in a distinctive 'soul' or 'identity'
and the 'laws that help manifest and maintain' its inner essence
constitute the '*dharma*' of the nation. Dharma, in this sense, is su
perior to the state. Particularly relevant in today's 'Ram Janam-

noomi' context are Deen Dayal's categorical statements that tradi-
ons are more important than Parliament, and that dharma cannot
e determined by plebiscite. 'True democracy', if it is to avoid li-
nse and conflict, has to combine freedom with dharma. There is
so a sharp attack on the federal aspects of the Indian constitution,
hich dilute the indivisibility of Bharat. Instead, there should be
ecentralization' giving more powers to village *panchayats*: how that
uld be combined with a strong unitary state was left admirably
gue.

Integral humanism seems to have been kept deliberately vague,
d this has helped it to plug into changing intellectual conditions.
darshan, who talked much more about integral humanism than
handari, described it as an effort to recover, in suitably modernized
rm, the alleged Hindu ideal of a multi-centred pluralist world.
his had been harmed by Islam, but damaged much more funda-
entally by Western forms of power and knowledge. British rule
ad brought in political and economic centralization, and the evils
ad been compounded by the Nehruvian model. The BJP ideal,
ated Bhandari, was decentralization through village *panchayats* as
ell as in economic life, and combined with the growth of a strong
ation, Gandhian socialism, he added, could be readily accommo-
ated within this framework.

If we compare the BJP discourse, as represented by Bhandari,
ith that of the RSS and the VHP, it appears to consist of a series
f politic qualifications that inadequately mask an underlying iden-
ty. The BJP probably needs both the mask—and its fairly apparent
nadequacy. Thus Bhandari disclaimed any intention to treat
Muslims as second-class citizens—but 'you are not permitted to be
ro-Pak,' and the 'pseudo-secular' placating of Muslims and dis-
rimination against Hindus must stop.' He repeated all the usual
harges against Muslims, but added as 'qualification' that 'the
Muslim, too, can be a gentleman': pseudo-secularist politicians are
uining him. Bhandari was obviously eager to emphasize the more
ecular aspects of his party's activities. The BJS and the BJP, he
aid, have always been 'political through and through', and have
ampaigned on any number of day-to-day political and economic
emands. But all these have only 'prepared the soil' for the crop,
nd now *barish* (rain) has come with Ram. Evident also was a desire

to disabuse us of any notion that the BJP was primarily a town an
trader-based party. Bhandari repeatedly talked of his party's wo
among peasants, starting with a campaign in the mid-1950s again
Nehru's plans to 'socialize' agriculture, right down to rural parti
ipation in the Ayodhya movement. The BJS, he told us, had wc
95 seats in UP in 1967, thanks to the Other Backward Classe
(OBC) support, but then Charan Singh took advantage of anti-Co
gress coalition politics to walk away with that stratum: an unwi
ting admission, of course, of the fragility of this rural base. Abou
the Mandal issue, Bhandari strongly favoured economic as again
caste-based reservation. He suddenly flew into a temper whe
probed a little further; evidently we had touched a sensitive spot

Twentieth century Hindutva had originated in middle cla
groups with a measure of modern education, and had little or r
connection for long with the world of traditional religious specia
ists—*sadhus* and *sants*, *mahants* and *purohits*. It was, therefore, a r
markably bold initiative of Golwalkar to organize a meeting o
Hindu religious leaders in Bombay in mid-1964 to discuss ways i
which various Hindu sects and tendencies could sink their mar
differences, work together, and establish contacts with Hindus re
siding abroad. Thus was laid the foundations of the Vishwa Hind
Parishad, and an RSS *pracharak*, Shivram Shankar Apte, became i
first general secretary. The subsequent career of the VHP, today th
most formidable of the RSS affiliates, demands a separate study, an
will be taken up in the next chapter.

THE RSS IN POLITICS: 60S TO 80S

The activist turn in the RSS from the early 1950s, manifeste
through the setting-up of affiliates, found expression also in occ
sional participation in movements that were more or less distar
from traditional RSS concerns. Thus Golwalkar assigned some *pro
charaks* to work with Vinoba Bhave, perhaps because the Bhooda
movement had as one of its context the Communist-led peasar
insurrection in Telengana. In 1954 RSS volunteers joined the *saty
graha* to liberate the Portuguese enclaves of Dadra and Nag
Haveli. This virtually unique RSS participation in an anti-coloni

ruggle seems to have been occasioned by the fear that Communists
ight come to dominate the movement. Relief work among East
engal refugees and 1950 Assam earthquake victims fitted in more
ith standard RSS traditions, while the campaign against cow-
aughter of 1952 provided an early opportunity for building con-
cts with traditional religious specialists. The RSS, however,
emained at a rather low ebb throughout the 1950s, and from 1956
o 1962 there were even moves for a retreat into pure character-
uilding. Eknath Ranade, general secretary during these years, tem-
orarily stopped the practice of sending *pracharaks* to work in
ffiliated organizations—a retreat opposed, significantly, by the
Deoras brothers, Balasaheb and Bhaurao.

The India-China war of 1962 inaugurated a sea-change in Indian
olitical life, with right-wing forces beginning to steadily gather
trength. A broad range of Left and centrist opinion, at times in-
luding Nehru himself, could now be branded for having been 'soft'
owards China, and the new respectability of the RSS was reflected
n the government permission given to it to participate as a separate
ontingent in the Republic Day parade of 1963. The RSS and the
an Sangh made full use of the 1965 Indo-Pak war to deepen sus-
icions about Muslims, and cashed in also on the growing unpop-
larity of the Congress wherever—as in the Hindi belt—the Left
lternative was weak or non-existent. The turn towards activism
outed through affiliates was conformed with the rapid rise in the
RSS hierarchy of Balasaheb Deoras, who became general secretary
n 1965, and succeeded Golwalkar as *sarsanghchalak* in 1973. Mean-
vhile the VHP had been floated, and connections with *sadhus*
trengthened, through a second, bigger and quite violent agitation
gainst cow-slaughter in 1967.

1967 also inaugurated an era in which the RSS's political affili-
te, already committed to agitational methods (justified by Deen
Dayal Upadhyay in his Presidential address of that year), decided to
trive for broad alliances with anti-Congress aims: a policy that had
very mixed results, many ups and downs, and occasioned much
nternal controversy. The RSS once again showed its flexibility by
acking a united front strategy which, for a time, in the short-lived
non-Congress governments of Bihar and UP in 1967, even included
Communists. Balraj Madhok, who had strongly opposed this policy,

was eventually pushed out of the BJS. The new importance give
by the RSS to electoral politics was reflected in its organization
changes in the early 1970s which made RSS units constituency
based. *Shakhas* now interested themselves directly in elections, n
only of legislatures, but also of trade unions, student and cultur
organizations. An early expression of this was the prominence
RSS *shakha pramukhs* in the elections to the Delhi University St
dents' Union and Delhi University Teachers' Association in 1973

RSS and BJS anti-Congress agitational politics reached a point
climax in the 1974–75 countrywide campaign against the Indi
Government led by Jayaprakash Narayan. JP and the RSS becam
for a while unexpected but close allies. Deoras hailed Jayaprakas
as a 'saint' in December 1974; the latter returned the complime
by publicly absolving the Jan Sangh of charges of fascism in Marc
1975; and, right on the eve of the Emergency, the Lok Sanghars
Samiti set up on 25 June 1975, chose Nanaji Deshmukh, form
RSS *pracharak* and top BJP leader, as its general secretary.

RSS attitudes under the Emergency revealed a curious duality
reminiscent of the 1948–49 days. The RSS (though not its affiliate
was banned, Deoras was arrested, and RSS sources claim that ter
of thousands of its members were imprisoned. It tried to organiz
a protest *satyagraha* between November 1975 and January 197
carried on some underground activities, and helped to organize th
Janata Party alliance prior to the 1977 elections. Yet Deoras in jai
like Golwalkar in 1948–49, quickly opened channels of commun
cation with the Emergency regime, writing fairly ingratiating le
ters to Indira Gandhi in August and November 1975 that promise
cooperation in return for a lifting of the ban. He tried to persuad
Vinoba Bhave to mediate between the RSS and the governmen
and sought also the good offices of Sanjay Gandhi. During the las
most reactionary phase of the Emergency, Indira Gandhi, too
seemed to have made some abortive overtures to the RSS, foreshad
owing the (partial) rapprochement between the Congress and Hind
communalism that would become quite evident in the 1980s.[33]

The Janata triumph of 1977 made RSS members central minis
ters for the first time (Vajpayee, Advani and Brijlal Verma). Fairl
soon, however, the history of the late 60s' anti-Congress coalition
started repeating itself. The Jan Sangh had formally surrendered it

identity to the Janata Party, but the question of 'dual member-ship'—former BJS members retaining obvious links with the RSS, which had steadfastly remained an independent body—became one of the issues which led to the Janata split in 1979. An interesting sidelight of these years was the blunt refusal by the RSS in August 1977 to open its membership to non-Hindus.

There had been 93 Jan Sangh MPs in the Janata majority of 1977, at the height of the anti-Congress wave; this went down to 16 in 1981, and the BJP, which was formed that year as reincarna-tion of the BJS, could get only two Parliamentary seats in the 1984 elections. The progress of the RSS organizationally, however, seems more or less unrelated to such electoral vicissitudes. The number of *shakhas* went up from 8500 in 1975 to 11,000 in 1977; it had risen to 20,000 by 1982, expanding particularly in the four southern states where it had been negligible earlier. A Government of India Home Ministry report in 1981 estimates the number of regular RSS participants at about a million, and financial contributions from members amounted to over Rs. 10 million annually.

The RSS by the early 1980s seems to have perfected its strategy of never keeping all its eggs in one basket. While the BJP remained fundamentally as tied to it as before, it developed some contacts with the Congress which, in Indira's last years, moved steadily to the right and displayed considerable eagerness to compete for the 'Hindu' vote in an increasingly opportunistic manner. There have been strong rumours that the BJP electoral debacle of 1984 was partly caused by the fact that the RSS switched some of its support to the Congress.

In the context of the breakup of the Janata alliance, Nanaji Desh-mukh in 1981 made a violent attack on parliamentary politics:

> Will it be possible to defeat the present immoral dictatorial tendencies in Indian politics through a resort to the power-oriented opportunistic and vote-getting politics?[34]

What this RSS attack heralded was not a return to unostentatious 'cultural' character-building, but a new premium on extra-parlia-mentary politics of an openly and aggressively Hindu communal type. A suitable instrument for this was already at hand, and, with the campaign against the Meenakshipuram conversions of that same

year, the VHP entered Indian politics in a big way, setting the scen
for the present Ram Janambhoomi movement.

NOTES

1. Achin Vanaik, 'The Enemy Within', *Sunday Review, Times of India*
   16 December 1990.
2. These include Anderson and Damle, *Brotherhood in Saffron*, New
   Delhi, 1987; J.A. Curran, *Militant Hinduism in Indian Politics: A
   Study of the RSS*, New York, 1951; M.S. Golwalkar, *Bunch of
   Thoughts*, Bangalore, 1966; Balraj Madhok, *Portrait of a Martyr*,
   Bombay, 1969; C.P. Bhishikar, *Keshav Sanghnirmata*, Pune, 1979
   (Hindi translation, Delhi, 1980); as well as a number of interviews
   referred to in the text. One of the few critical accounts of the RSS
   which provided us with valuable insights into this organization, is
   the book *Rashtriya Swayamsevak Sangh* (New Delhi, 1979) written
   by ex-*swayamsevak* D.R. Goyal.
3. Bhishikar, 1979, p. 7.
4. *Ibid.*, p. 25.
5. K.S. Sudarshan, Joint General Secretary of the RSS, proudly recalled
   this idea of Nevedita in the interview he gave us.
6. Bhishikar, 1979, pp. 43–44.
7. See, for instance, the extracts from the Venugopal Commission Report (1982) on the Kanyakumari Hindu-Christian riots in *Mainstream*, 22 June 1991.
8. Bhishikar, 1979, p. 98.
9. Pyarelal, *Mahatma Gandhi: The Last Phase*, Ahmedabad, p. 440.
10. G.D. Tendulkar, *Mahatma*, Volume III, Bombay, 1945, pp. 130–34.
11. Balraj Madhok, 1969, pp. 28–29.
12. J.A. Curran, 1951, pp. 18–19.
13. *Ibid.*, p. 19.
14. Bhishikar, 1980, p. 30.
15. M.S. Golwalkar, *We or Our Nationhood Defined*, Nagpur, 1938, p. 27.
16. *Ibid.*, p. 52.
17. Golwalkar, 1966, pp. 123–24.
18. *Ibid.*, pp. 127–28.
19. *Ibid.*, p. 128.
20. *Organiser*, February 2, 1962.
21. *Organiser*, June 10, 1963.

22. *Organiser*, January 4, 1970.
23. *Organiser*, June 3, 1979.
24. Golwalkar, 1966, pp. 142–43.
25. Quoted in RSS pamphlet *Justice on Trial: A Collection of the Historic Letters between Sri Guruji and the Government*, Bangalore, 1968, pp. 23–26.
26. Golwalkar, 1966, pp. 333–34.
27. *Ibid.*, p. 350.
28. C.A. Bayly, *Rulers, Townsmen and Bazaars: North Indian Society in the age of British Expansion, 1770–1870*, Cambridge, 1983, p. 8 and chapters 10, 11.
29. *Organiser*, April 8, 1979.
30. Golwalkar, 1966, p. 335.
31. Interview with Acharya Giriraj Kishore.
32. For more details, see Tanika Sarkar, 'The Women as Communal Subject: Rashtrasevika Samiti and Ramjanmabhoomi Movement', *Economic and Political Weekly*, XXVI-35, 31 August 1991.
33. Andersen and Damle, 1987, p. 213.
34. *Ibid.*, p. 227.

3

The VHP: Organizing Mass Communalism

THE VHP PHASE OF HINDUTVA

The Hindutva of today constitutes a major departure from previous phases of Hindu communal mobilization in one crucial respect. Unlike earlier periods of acute communal tension (in the 1890s, the 1920s, the 40s or the 60s) it is inseparably identified with a concrete organizational complex. Earlier communalization did depend on organizational inspiration as well, but the VHP (and the larger institutional structure that it is tied to) has made itself co-extensive with the phenomenon of mass communalism.

This is done through staking out a new and a very large claim. The movement it leads is supposed not only to represent the vanguard, the politically aware elite within Hindu society (this would have been, roughly, the earlier RSS claim): it asserts that it *already* includes the whole of Hindu society as it stands here and now, and that an exact correspondence exists between its own field and the boundaries of an admittedly varied, pluralistic, differentiated Hindu world.

An important way of staking this claim is to assert an identity of interest with a broad range of Hindu organizations that are officially distinct from itself. The VHP does not claim oneness with very different and historically distinct bodies to simply demonstrate its leadership over them. It makes these diverse institutions stand in for a pluralistic Hindu society. Claims of identity with them then gets easily translated into claims of full powers of representation over the entire Hindu world.

The claim has important practical implications. Having asserted it often and forcefully enough, the VHP can then present its own commands and injunctions as Hindu collective will. Each Hindu can be told authoritatively that all Hindus feel the need to arm themselves against Muslims, not because the VHP tells them to do so, but because the whole community so desires. Not only is the relationship with the Muslims altered, but Hindus are then made to look at their own religion in very different ways. The centrality given to Ram worship, for instance, crucially ruptures, devotional patterns in non-Hindi belt regions. In Bengal, while a particular version of the *Ramayana* is a familiar and cherished epic, there is no tradition of Ram temples or Ram worship as such, the chief deities being Durga-Kali and Krishna in different forms. By making the devotional traditions of north Indian Hindus obligatory upon all Hindus everywhere, regional and local patterns of belief are being arbitrarily violated. The claim of today's Hindutva to an immediate identity with the entire Hindu world thus conceals and legitimizes the operations of an intrusive, authoritarian political formation which defines not only the Muslim, but also the Hindu solely in its own terms. A deeply undemocratic syllogism follows: Hindus are the majority, the RSS-BJP-VHP combine has the unique power of defining what being a Hindu means, and therefore, the will of this political formation must prevail on a permanent basis.

In the course of this section, we shall explore some of the crucial ways in which the VHP seeks this self-image: through its organizational apparatus, its popularization of the RSS world-view, and its strategies.

Our exploration in areas adjoining Nizamuddin after the riot there in March 1990[1] forcibly brought home to us the coming together of very diverse Hindu organizations which is such a striking feature of the present, VHP phase of Hindutva. At the Arya Samaj Mandir at Jangpura, we were directed towards the Sanatan Dharm Mandir by a Samaj official who said that *sanatanists* would expound the same basic principles. The late nineteenth to early twentieth century heritage of bitter Arya-Sanatani conflict seemed utterly forgotten. At the Dharm Mandir *pujaris* told us that their Lajpat Nagar premises are shared by the VHP. At the Namdev Temple Samiti office on Lodi Road, we came across busy mobilization for a march under VHP auspices which would protest against a recent judgement of the US Supreme Court against ISKCON (International Society for Krishna Consciousness) properties. On Ram Navami day in April 1990, we saw trucks sporting VHP placards in front and Arya Samaj ones at the back. *Rashtrasevikas* told us that all VHP, Arya Samaj or Sanatan Dharm premises were freely available for their activities. The RSS-run Saraswati Shishu Mandir at Naraina Vihar in Delhi has the identical architectural layout and visual design as the DAV school at Yusuf Sarai: a central icon of *Bharatmata* is flanked on both sides by wall frescoes of Hindu nationalist or legendary heroes, of wars with Muslims. Each organization told us that 1925 was the key moment for Hindu awakening: all explained subsequently that the RSS was born that year. 'We are all Hindus, we are all the same,' every spokesman of each organization recited at the beginning of their exposition. All of them reduced differences in beliefs and practices to personal idiosyncrasies. None claimed an exclusive monopoly over the fundamental truth of Hinduism.

This could well be a purely temporary tactical coordination. Yet it has already introduced a qualitatively new concept of Hindu unity. A whole history of conflicting paths and resolutions has been freed of real difference. Historical plurality is substituted by the political myth of an unvarying common fight against the Muslim.

The claim of the VHP to represent the entire Hindu space has an important temporal dimension. Earlier Hindu communal organizations that aimed at mobilizing society would assume a time-lag between the foundation of the organization and the realization of its aims. There would be some notion of an intervening historical process through which the organization would come to enfold society within itself. In effect the time lag implied an intermediate stage of self-reform. Late nineteenth century revivalists had set out to work for certain basic doctrinal transformations within Hinduism. Even though the organizational drive of the 20s had divested itself of any insistence on a uniform, reformed doctrine or practice, a trace of the earlier imperative persisted. The RSS or the Hindu Mahasabha saw themselves as the nucleus of an organized militant society of the future. *Sangh samaj me sangathan nahi, samaj ka sangathan hai* (the Sangh is not an organization in society, it is the organization of society), proclaimed an RSS pamphlet.[2] Yet even this assumes a deferring of fulfillment. If *samaj* does not need to reform itself, it still needs to be organized by the RSS—something that lies in the future. The present departure resides in the fact that the presumed time-lag between aspiration and realization has been completely erased. Ram's birthplace still needs to be won back and Hindu Rashtra must replace the secular state. Yet the organization and the *samaj* are already one: no internal transformation is required.

A tremendous self-multiplication of the core organizational cluster is used to confirm this suggestion. The RSS strategy of continuous export of trained cadres from the mother organization to an expanding range of affiliates and sub-affiliates had already paved the way for that. The VHP itself brought in its wake a whole range of dynamic, subsidiary fronts. Each of them was used during the RJB movement to indicate a breakthrough into varied social level—women, youths, *sadhus*—until it seemed that nothing was left that was not in the movement. A planned coordination that deliberately organized a phased self-multiplication, was presented as spontaneous participation by new ranks of Hindus, the mutual conjoining of society and organization. The movement thus appeared as rooted in an unmediated social will rather than in the directives of an organization. This consequently added immense authority to its anti-secular and anti-Muslim commands.

This was sought to be realized by a rather unusual strategy—that of steadfastly refusing claims to originality and innovation, of continuously dispersing its sources of inspiration as widely as possible among authorities who are distant, even antagonistic—Rabindranath, Gandhi, Bhagat Singh, Ambedkar. No great Hindu figure has been wasted. Rather than composing a distinct, defined lineage for itself, the attempt is to establish a complex, constantly proliferating and sprawling kinship network which stops only at the Muslim, the Christian and the 'secular'. At the same time, the great figures are frozen into static icons and their specific ideas and messages are left unpacked. Pluralism is made into a spectacle through a process of co-option which never spells out the grounds for appropriation: how

Rabindranath, Gandhi, Bhagat Singh and Ambedkar could conceivably be pulled into the orbit of Hindu Rashtra would have been an impossible question to answer, and hence cannot be raised at all.

Since the VHP claims to have appropriated all Hindus, signs of this occupation have to be made visible all over the Hindu world. The movement therefore works its way from the overtly political domain into everyone's everyday life, primarily through the innovative use of small icons, derived from calendar art: the sticker, the slogan, the *bhagwa dhwaj*. During the *kar seva* campaign, all Hindu households were required to fly—and a very large number of urban as well as rural households in U.P. did fly—the saffron flag. The most interesting specimen in this connection was the sticker displaying Ram and/or the temple. Slickly produced in a variety of garish colours, at one time they could be seen all over North Indian cities and towns and also in many villages. They could be pasted anywhere—on vehicles, offices, houses, or on school blackboards. Their reach extended much beyond that of posters or wall-writing. They swamped individuals in their ubiquity, contriving a sense of the irresistible tide of Hindutva.

This was no spontaneous upsurge of popular devotional creativity. For one thing, the concerted and expensive process of production required a high level of planning and investment. A. Shankar's *Warning: India in Danger* (VHP publication) that was promoted at least six months before the small icons swept into the market, is a booklet which asks each reader to xerox and distribute copies of itself among at least twenty more people. It also provides a blueprint about how and why Ram messages could occupy the entire visual space of Hindus. It advises the putting up of prominent hoardings 'highlighting Hindu principles', universal display of saffron flags, use of the *om* symbol on doors and vehicles and wearing of '*om* lockets'. The point then is not simply the ubiquity of Hindutva symbols but a monopoly of their production in VHP hands. Unlike visuals used by other political groups, the VHP does not put its visible signature on its products. What it does is to use a distinctive format (say the coupling of Ram and the yet to be built *mandir*), which identifies it as the work of the VHP, at the same time as it symbolizes a 'non-partisan' symbol of Hindu aspirations and self-identification.

Not only is production prolific but messages are made to reinforce each other, develop each other's meeting in an ascending spiral. The need to create a self-referential system of images and meanings is important since Hindutva works through several interrelated organizations and is engaged with changing political objectives over a fairly long period of time. When elections approach, for instance, the BJP takes over the sticker culture from the VHP and develops the theme of Ram Mandir into a call for Ram Rajya. A popular election slogan in 1991, for instance, was: *Ram rajya ki ore chale/Bhajpa ke saath chale* (Lets go towards Ram Rajya, lets move with the BJP). The VHP itself coordinates its images with contemporary middle class aspirations. The most familiar iconic rendering of the Ayodhya temple on a poster is one where the warrior Ram is displayed on the left corner at the top. The centre is filled with a pseudo-photographic depiction of the non-existent temple, designed by a descendant of the architect who had rebuilt the Somnath temple on North Indian *nagari* rather than on South Indian architectural lines (we were told this by the VHP *sanyasi* Giriraj Kishore). The future construction is projected as an already-realized, existing present, typifying once again the basic VHP strategy of effacing the distance between aspiration and fulfilment. On the right-hand corner at the bottom, the present tense is embodied in the shape of a blue Maruti car which substitutes for human devotees. The spectacle is indeed worthy of the Hindutva of twenty-first century consumerism—a living expression of the fetishization and commodification of human devotion.

The successful elaboration of the self-referential network of usable and portable messages is dependent on the deployment of a limited range of basic symbols: Ram (as a baby, and as armed adult), the temple, *om*, the saffron flag. A danger exists, however, that their target group need not necessarily accept the desired single message, especially since the symbols are traditional ones, loaded with older and different meanings. Asked if he had joined the 'Ram party', a New Delhi *panwala*, who had a sticker pasted on his cigarette cupboard in the shop, gestured at the image of the *mandir* and said, 'I don't want this,' and then pointing to the figure of Ram in the foreground declared, 'I have kept this for him.' Stickers use traditional religious symbols in a constituency that is increasingly making distinctions between politics and religion. They still represent, however, a major advance in the dissemination of the VHP world-view, for the ubiquity of small icon tries to transform their character from objects of worship (an *om* sign on a car, or a picture of Ram stuck to a bus stand, can hardly be that) to signs of one's Hindu identity.

The VHP carefully regulates the production of variations on the same theme. Take, for instance, the figure of Ram in two poses, apparently very different from each other. In one an apocalyptic leader is silhouetted against a purple sky, his torso and legs uncovered, his hair and loincloth flowing against a raging storm. This is Ram the disinherited, radiating a mood of elemental anger. In the other image he stands against a bright golden temple with an *om* inscribed on the blue sky above. his smiling face is almost feminine in sweetness, his body is laden with jewels. The viewer is offered two choices: Ram the warrior, fighting for his rights in a battle that signifies apocalyptic upheaval, and Ram the king, embodiment of a golden age of Hindu culture, source of stability and reassurance. Yet both share two fundamental aspects—his weapons and his single presence, uncluttered with additional figures. Whatever else he may mean, Ram, above all, symbolizes martial prowess. His weapons are his only companions, sustaining him in both disinheritance and glory. While Ram as a Kshatriya king is rightfully a warrior figure, the new element that makes all the difference here is the unstated reference to the fact that the weapons are meant for the destruction of the Muslims. The message is simultaneously conveyed and affirmed by so many other forms of VHP propaganda that it need not be added to the icon itself explicitly, but will, nonetheless, continue to frame its reception.

The small icons that insinuate themselves in the daily lives of Hindus, arise out of and create a basis for larger symbolic actions. Since the early '80s, when the VHP came into its own in North India, it has invented a series of political rituals that were meant to encompass every corner and each individual of Hindu India—the sacrifices and the *yatras* (*Ekmata Yajna* in 1983, *Shri Ramjanaki Janambhoomi Yatra* in 1984, several other *rath yatras* in 1985–89, the *Shila Pujan* and *Shilanyas* ceremonies at Ayodhya in 1989, and finally, Advani's *rath yatras* in 1990). While some are consciousness-raising tours, others require active contributions from everyone—a brick, a rupee, or the sale of a bottle of Ganga water in each village of the country. It is a way of claiming, and, to an extent, creating, oneness—always under VHP auspices. Interestingly, the human devotee is yet again embodied in a brick or a rupee that he/she has sent or the bottle of holy water he/she has purchased: i.e., devotion is ultimately translated into money. The rituals, moreover, are spread over months and are continuously innovative. Through them, Ram's saga is transcreated for contemporary consumption where the *rath* becomes a dressed-up DCM Toyota van.

The VHP creates its own form of oneness through a new calendar of Hindu festivals that also includes some Scheduled Caste (especially Valmiki and Ravidas *pujas*), Sikh and Buddhist sacred events. Altogether, it seems to sum up the entire span of Hindu festive activity. Noticeably, oneness is not projected as sameness, or a fundamentalist commitment to an identical body of doctrine and practice, but through its reverse. It is achieved through a controlled pluralism, through a single organizational cluster that allows yet coordinates a large range of sacred events.

The most striking aspect of small icons and new rituals that virtually substitute Ram and his temple for all other Hindu practices and symbols, is that they have made Ram irrevocably associated not with Ravana in a 'Manichaean' world-view, but with Babur and Muslim rule. The new historical myths have achieved this vital substitution of associative feeling so silently and effectively that in the icons and festivals, the Muslim need not be introduced at all, and so the established iconic format need not be disturbed. Ram's face and his life story are enough to release a chain of associations that has detached itself from all known epic narratives and brought in the invented medieval history of India.

Pluralism in VHP discourse translates into many ways of experiencing pleasure—once again introducing a consumerist imperative. Sudarshan spent a long time enumerating, with relish, the rich variety of practices among different Hindus, ranging from strict mutual monogamy to even polyandry. Acharya Giriraj Kishore frankly described the many differences among the Shankaracharyas all of whom however, bless the cause of the temple. The *rashtra-sevikas* maintained that there were no compulsory observances for women. There was tolerance, good humour, celebration in such references. At the same time, Giriraj Kishore was speechless when we insisted on an answer to our query: what happens when two mutually exclusive practices confront each other? For instance, when harijans are massacred by upper castes because of accidental pollution through physical touch? Which side would the VHP be on? Girirajji's silence pointed out that the VHP can describe diversity only as a higher form of harmony, and never as a source of conflict. For it, differences are not structured by oppression and violence, they co-exist in the departmental stores of Hindutva as a row of attractive packages.

VHP Organization

Behind the VHP's claim to incorporate everything within itself lies a subtle restructuring of the individual units as well as the general shape of the Hindu world. For the very first time, an ecumenical order is being sought to be imposed upon Hinduism. It is necessary, therefore, to have a closer look at the VHP organizational structure. The VHP was born in 1964 when Golwalkar, on behalf of the RSS, met a select group of *sanyasis* and heads of religious organizations in Bombay to start a new mass front which was supposed to unite all Hindu religious sects under a single umbrella. For the first ten years the new organization worked largely in the North Eastern States, proselytizing against Christian missionaries. After the Meenakshipuram incident of 1981 when some harijans converted to Islam, its focus was turned against Muslims. In this new phase, it sought to enlarge and formalize the institutional links with men of religion across the country. Two apex bodies were created for religious leaders—the Marg Darshak Mandal, meeting once or twice annually, and the Dharm Sansad which meets only when needed. Shankaracharyas—the heads of top ranking *maths*—were given a prominent role within them and most of them became closely identified with VHP politics.

Such linkages with *sadhus* and *sants* are crucial, for they give to Hindutva the platform by which it can be seen as part of the long and popular history of Hinduism itself. The *sanyasis* become the vehicle to articulate Hindutva's ambition of organizing a Hindu identity and State. At Bilhaur (central U.P.) just before the elections in 1991, we met a *sanyasi* from the Bandra forest area who told us that he had read Savarkar at the age of ten. When asked to define a Hindu, he repeated Savarkar's definition verbatim. The movement to 'liberate' the three *janambhoomis* was initiated through two *dharm sansads* held in 1984 and 1985. The VHP video cassettes focus long on their deliberations, suggesting that their demands spring from an urgent devotional necessity. The transaction was a two ways one, and the VHP put some specific interest of religious organizations on their agenda: most notably the freeing of temple managements from government control.

Legally, the VHP was conceived of as a trust, with a 100-member Board of Trustees and a 51-strong Governing Council. The latter body includes only one *sanyasi* at present, Swami Chinmayananda— an indication, perhaps, that the ultimate controlling power rests not with traditional religious leaders, but with RSS cadres. As a trust cannot enroll members directly, VHP activists are called *hitchintaks* (well-wishers).

The trust, in course of time, has developed eighteen departments, and even a mere enumeration of their purposes provides a clue to the range of VHP activities and aspirations. There is a Dharma Anusthan department organizing *kirtans* and *bhajans* in temples. Another branch looks after the missionary, or *dharma prachar* work, geared to the 'reconversion' of Christians and Muslims. Yet another is the Acharya Vibhag which trains *pujaris* for the VHP as well as for many non-VHP run temples. The Parva Samanuyaya department coordinates common festivals with non-VHP temple committees. A VHP leaflet listed 72 such organizations in Delhi, including Sana-tanis, the Arya Samaj, Sikh Sanghs, several Buddhist and Jain bod-ies, and Valmiki Mandir Committees from among harijan groups. By expanding in such ways its influence among the *pujari* network and also by setting up or acquiring temples of its own, the VHP clears the way for a common set of deities, rituals, sacred occasions, all with the explicit purpose of initiating a common fight against the Muslims, the demand of Hindu Rashtra.

At the heart of the huge VHP complex at Ramakrishna Puram in Delhi lies a Hanuman temple that preceded the VHP construction. The *pujari* has lately affiliated himself to the VHP and the old temple space is going to be overshadowed by a large new sanctum with *Bharat Mata* as its central icon. There is also a department on *maths* and *mandirs* that coordinates activities among different religious establishments. Another department looks after Sanskrit education and provides a ten-day crash course in spoken and written Sanskrit. The VHP has announced its intention of reviving Sanskrit as a living Indian language, since all the crucial *samskar*-forming texts are in Sanskrit. For the VHP, however, the Sanskrit treasure trove is not constituted by either classical literature or the philosophies, but primarily by prescriptive texts. *Manusmriti* and *Arthashastra* are taken to be specially central to the idea of Hindu Rashtra. It is interesting to remember that the *Manusmriti* prescribes a rigidity stratified caste and gender hierarchy, while the *Arthashastra* recommends a police state under a single despotic head. These remain live and valid traditions for the VHP. Doordarshan too extended its cooperation to the project by initiating the long serial "Chanakya", based on the life of the putative author of *Arthashastra*.

Alongside such branches oriented towards mobilizing and training high caste religious specialists, the VHP also has a service department which works mainly among harijans and tribals, especially in forest areas. Picking up from a rather scanty network of RSS welfare organizations, the VHP first developed them in the sixties and the seventies mainly among the Christian tribals of the North-East. Later they were extended to Delhi, Karnataka, Orissa, Andhra Pradesh, M.P., Tamil Nadu, Maharashtra, Kerala, U.P. and Bihar. The 'Hinduization' of exploited social groups became urgent, particularly after the Meenakshipuram incident.[3] There are recent plans of working among backward caste peasants of U.P. and Bihar, but so far the accent has largely been on forest tribes: relatively isolated, marginal, and less integrated with formed caste hierarchies. A *sadhu* from the Banda forest area of U.P. told us that the VHP are in constant touch with the forest-dwelling Kol tribes. The form of VHP activity among such groups reveals the significant influences of the RSS model. It is mainly educational work, setting up libraries, *yogashramas*, *balwadis*, student hostels and child *samskar* centres for developing knowledge of Hindu texts and Hindu national heroes. There is some provision for vocational training for small-scale employment projects; but the central thrust—though seldom described as such—is clearly a 'conversion' of tribals and harijans to recognizably respectable Hindutva forms of worship. Upper caste RSS youths at Bilhaur described tribals and harijans as 'dirty and ignorant', who can now join Hindu society by contributing to Ram's cause. VHP workers give Ram icons to Kol tribes in Banda, and Raghunandan Prasad Sharma's *VHP: Aims, Activities and Achievements* advises the spread of the 'chief religious *samskaras*' among '*vanavasis, girijans* and *harijans*'. Clearly these are meant to replace existing beliefs and practices among tribals and ensure a homogenized version of religion. Equally clearly these three categories are seen not really to belong and must earn that right. There is no provision for any circulation of beliefs or practices from these levels to mainstream Hindus, not a hint of any perception that *adivasi* traditions may conceivably have something worth preserving or adding on to Brahminical Hinduism.

The rhetoric about the equal validity of plural custom within a wide and tolerant Hindu world thus breaks down. At bottom, tribal and lower caste practices and beliefs are treated with Brahminical contempt and suspicion,   a distortion that needs to be corrected. It is significant also that in recent years the interest in tribals seems to have moved away from the North-East to areas where tribals have been waging class and political struggles under left-leaning groups—the Bastar region in M.P. or Chotanagpur in Bihar, for instance. To the overarching imperative of insulating tribals and forest people from the attraction of Islam and Christianity is added a social imperative of creating a base and movement among them which would be violently activist but which will not question the politics of the social and economic marginalization of these tribes.

A third category of VHP work is more directly agitational. There is, for instance, a department of cow protection, which continues the older *sanatani* tradition of *go-shalas* but functions now primarily as a confrontational body. It agitates against the legalized sale of beef in Kerala and West Bengal. The Bajrang Dal (BD) department looks after the training of young boys. It calls itself by different names in different parts of the country. In Bengal for instance, it is known as the Vivekananda Vahini. The department of Durga Vahini is its counterpart among young girls. Both are primarily urban with a significant reach within small towns in U.P., and draw their recruits from young people with regular leisure time and some financial security. Unlike the RSS they do not have regular *shakha* training, but organize seven-day camps every year. Their centres are located at Hanuman Mandirs where they organize weekly *satsangs*. Lacking a regular ideological or physical training programme, or fixed schedule for activities which still remain the preserve of the RSS, they seem to constitute really a reserve force for agitational activities. A BD activist described the department as an organ for the 'protection of Hindus', that is, by definition they come alive only in times of conflict with Muslims. They were largely instrumental in recruiting urban youths for the *kar sevas* at Ayodhya. The *rashtrasevikas* told us that they had provided martial arts training to the Durga Vahini at that point. At the VHP rally of April 4, 1991 in Delhi, we talked to a group of local Bajrang Dal youths who were somewhat inarticulate about their aims and programmes. Then Pramath Pandey from Bhilai explained that the Dal teaches youths 'how to be Hindus and how to obey instructions'. Vikas, a young RSS member from Shahdara, Delhi, intervened to say that the Dal is instructed in disciplined work by the RSS. He then filled in Pramath's hesitant comments by telling us that the Dal's main ideal is, 'not to retreat and they believe in tit for tat', once again confirming that the Dal functions largely in conflict situations.

After the BJP assumed power in Uttar Pradesh the latest skirmishes on the Ayodhya issue featured BD activists directly, while the BJP, RSS and even the VHP shunned a public posture. A subaffiliate can thus be deployed to keep an issue alive for future use while the more important fronts can remain relatively quiet so that the issue is not highlighted beyond a point, to create embarrassment to the BJP government. The fact that the BD is known to recruit untrained, volatile, semi-lumpen elements in contrast to the handpicked and thoroughly-coached RSS cadres also absolves the larger front and core organizations from direct responsibility for reckless acts of indiscipline or violence. But the BD was clearly straining at the leash and the VHP, equally clearly, did not mean to expand the scope of their action in the immediate future. Signs of strain were all too evident.

The Matri Mandal department is the affiliate that works among older women. It started operating in Delhi from the early eighties and has now about 500 members. The rate of growth has been quite low compared to the radical Delhi based women's organizations. It promotes *Samskar Kendras* among small children aged between five and ten. It also undertakes some charity work, especially in large urban hospitals. Krishna Sharma, who heads the Delhi *mahila* wing and who is married to B.L. Sharma, described how their workers regularly visit critically ill people in several hospitals, comfort relatives in distress and prepare food for those patients who do not receive delicacies from homes. Significantly, no special work is promoted by this department for women's rights. Instead of regular group meetings they pay informal visits to each other's homes. The work is low key, distanced from various problems, not geared to rapid expansion. The real purpose seems to be the training of workers in related but minor frontline work.

The foreign coordination committee believes that Hindus all over the world constitute a single country which is then divided up among 30 odd 'branches'. There are a few technical departments that look after finance, publications and administration work. The most influential departments at the moment are the propaganda and Ram Janambhoomi *vibhags* (departments).

Through the VHP, the RSS has made a significant break from its own past. The Hindu that the earlier RSS sought to construct was surely grounded in a known religion; yet, the definition of that religion itself was overtly cultural and implicitly political. Prior to the VHP, the ecclesiastical institutions within Hindu society were left scrupulously alone while fronts were built up among most lay sections—women, workers, students, kisans. But today we find the flourishing Mataji temple near the Jhandewalla RSS office being run by an RSS-dominated board of trustees. Some *sanyasis* from Basti related how they had overhauled regular readings of sacred texts (*kathas*) at temples to include taped messages of Sadhvi Rithambara. With the VHP bridgehead into organized religion, the RSS has, at last, filled up a crucial gap for itself. Its claims to all of Hinduism is consequently fuller and more confident. 'Even the *sanyasis* are rising in defence of RJB,' thundered Rithambara and she was echoed by all the important *sants* at the last Dharm Sansad at Delhi in April 1991. The message has two implications. Since, within a traditional

Hindu world view, renouncers have a special claim over truth and wisdom even about the mundane world, their authority is supreme and their summons cannot be ignored. Equally, their participation reveals beyond doubt that the entire Hindu world was within the present movement, and that violence against Muslims was a sacred duty, prescribed by *sanyasis*. During October 1990, house and temple walls at Ayodhya and Faizabad displayed slogans that said 'it is the compulsory religious duty of Hindus to *kill* those who kill cows' (emphasis ours). The involvement of ascetics in the movement ensured that the injunction was issued by the proper authorities.

The agenda—from training *pujaris* in proper Sanskrit and *samskaras* to constructing a single hierarchical structure with an apex body in the Dharm Sansad—relies on, draws in and changes the traditional temple, *math*, and Shankaracharya networks. Simultaneously it reorders the traditional priorities within Hindu piety by imposing its own circuit of new pilgrimage sites. While Giriraj Kishore acknowledged the sanctity of older sacred sites like Gaya and Puri, he was clearly not very enthusiastic about them. The major spots, according to him were Somnath, Benaras, Mathura and, above all, Ayodhya. He explained the principle behind the hierarchy; 'The other ones had not been destroyed by Muslims.' It was, therefore, the association with violence and conflict in past and present that conferred sanctity. The struggle for the RJB is also the VHP's struggle for the conquest of Hinduism.

The break from the past agenda is, nevertheless, only partial. There is a dialectic between the present sense of a surfeit and the traditionally austere boundaries of the RSS. While initiating and identifying with the new move, the RSS still retains its organizational autonomy and the old agenda, albeit within the broader movement that it has created around itself. The VHP derives all its *pracharaks* from the RSS. Its entire ideological and organizational apparatus, therefore, remains under RSS supervision. Like creatures which encase themselves and breed within a protective outer covering provided by their own saliva, the RSS continues its molecular model of cultural change and character formation.

IDEOLOGY AND SOCIAL COMPOSITION

Hindutva at this moment is in a triumphalist mood, having emerged ideologically and electorally as a viable alternative to the Gandhi-Nehru legacy of a democratic State, professing adherence to social welfare and multi-culturalism. Even global events these days, with the rapid dismantling of the Second World along with the crisis that faces socialist theory, seem to confirm and add to its claims. The emphasis on the collapse of non-capitalist orders—especially marked in RSS-VHP expositions of the past two years—underlines, all the more strongly, the relatively hidden agenda of Hindutva which is directed against socialism. Doctrinally, socialism is more disturbing for Hindutva than the ideology of Islam, for the RSS-VHP world-view is singularly ill-equipped to deal with questions of social conflict. Its own argument poses no alternative socio-economic perspective that can possibly cope with the fundamental questions of inequality and exploitation raised by socialist doctrines. Hence its recent pronouncements like Sudarshan's speech on April 4 on the one hand, continues the old assertion of *Integral Humanism* that materialism is spiritually impoverishing; on the other hand, a fresh empirical weight is added by pointing to the collapse of the Second World, which relieves Hindutva of directly replying to the doctrinal challenge of socialism.[4]

Just as socialism is conveniently pigeonholed into a crude and limited this-worldliness and some failed historical systems, there is similarly, neither an adequate theory of capitalism nor its critique. Capitalism is seen as yet another form of materialism, equally based on the notion of mutual conflict against which a non-analysed idea of harmony is counterpoised. At the same time, while its competitive and materialist nature is rhetorically condemned, the labour relations and forms of social organization generated by that order are implicitly accepted. New generations of the Hindu Right are obviously to work diligently within them and benefit accordingly. In Upadhyaya's *Integral Humanism* there was a small, undeveloped reference to hedonistic consumption and the consequent depletion of natural resources. Interestingly, recent writings have shifted the focus to a more trans-social notion of a rather crude form of ecology, which traces the spoliation of nature to the innate character of

Western scientific man and to his desire to conquer nature. The delinking of ecological problems from consumerist capitalism constitutes an absent argument[5] which is illustrative of the relevance of new Hindutva for a diasporic, urban, business-oriented, booming global formation fueled by consumerist desires and opportunities. The counter-order is located in a superior 'scientific' organic understanding within traditional Hinduism which structures man within, and not against nature. Hindutva today is in a self-congratulatory mood. While *Integral Humanism* did concede that Western science has something to teach us, more recent RSS-VHP publications are more at pains to establish that Western scientists themselves are rediscovering the relevance of Hindu social, physical and human sciences.[6]

'Western' social orders, whether in the First or the Second World are claimed to be equally premised on mutual conflict and competition rather than on harmony and organic links, and being entirely materialistic, they constitute a relatively underdeveloped notion of social existence. Significantly, problems of individual freedom, civil rights or democracy within the Second World, or of exploitation, alienation and commodification of all human relations under capitalism, are pushed aside. In a move that suggests lineages in the third path (neither communism nor capitalism) that national socialism in Germany had set itself, Hindutva's simplistic constructs of the 'West' are meant to provide foils to the construction of a 'Hindu' order. Presumably the sources of this idyllic alternative comes from actual historical experience. Yet nowhere are these 'Hindu' values historicized or historically proved: they are simply pulled in random fashion as contrasts and are made to co-exist continuously as a seamless whole for a supposed 'Hindu history'.

Given the centrality of the ideal model of Hindu values, it is curious to find a persistent inability to see it in terms of different historical periods. 'Hindu history' is always pushed back into the mythic world. History, for B.L. Sharma, really begins with Muslim invasions. Everything that went before is taken to be an undifferentiated, unchanging continuation of Ram Rajya. While the historically unspecified 'Hindu period' acts as a repository of stable symbols, within ancient history as a whole, a sort of a break is introduced through the notion of Buddhist 'states' and their supposed neglect of Hindu temples and martial valour.[7] The RSS plans to bring out a multi-volume history of India. The only volume on which work has so far begun is the Buddhist period. Even though rhetorically, Buddhism is made a part of Hinduism, in practice the interpretation of Buddhist historical experience present as a disaster that emasculated the ancient 'Hindu nation'. All departures from an animal slaughter centred Brahminism and imperial ambitions are thereby implicitly condemned, and a justification is provided for the extermination of Buddhism within its birthplace. At the same time, an aggressive warrior ethos is made into an immutable, absolute 'Hindu' value, from which any change would be undesirable. So while the core of 'Hindu' philosophy is made out to be peace and tolerance (and, a contrast is made with other world religions which supposedly lack these qualities), the ideal value of the historical Hindu is taken to be military glory. This way the best of both worlds is ensured: gloating about a superior tolerance, while confirming the necessity for its own violent and aggressive agenda.

On the eve of the *kar seva* programme, Rithambara proclaimed an immediate, all-out war: *'khoon kharaba hota hai to ek bar hone do'* (if there has to be bloodshed let it happen once and for all), impatient to pulverize an already battered minority community, her longings not yet satisfied by Meerut, Maliana, Bhagalpur, Ahmedabad, Banaras and Kanpur. *Angry Hindu! Yes. Why not? Why are Hindus in the Dock?* exhorts the title of an RSS booklet, celebrating lethal anger as the saving grace for the community. A Hindu Jagaran Manch leaflet from Khurja evokes the image of divine vengeance seeking Muslim blood, thereby transposing revenge from the political need of a human community to the desire of the gods: *'Ranchandi khali khappar liye gali gali vichar rahi hai'* (the goddess of war is roaming around the lanes looking for blood).

While the image of the angry, rampant Hindu gets translated into reality like a self-fulfilling prophecy, so grows the emphasis on the notions of tolerance, peace and 'real' secularism in the Hindutva discourse. We have already referred to the repeated expositions of Hindu pluralism. Hindu Rashtra, structured by this principle, therefore offers maximum security to other faiths, says a VHP booklet, *Why Hindu Rashtra?*. Secularism in its internal principle, is supposedly contained within the definition of the Hindu Rashtra

73

itself, and 'pseudo-secularists' only want to subvert this potential. In our investigations among a wide range of people in Delhi, especially among school teachers deeply influenced by the RSS, we often came across a particular sentence: 'Of course we love the Muslim, we love even insects.' 'Even Muslims have their gentlemen and Islam has produced its own civilizations,' Bhandari had assured us. Ram Swarup's subtly persuasive arguments ground this reassurance on claims to a philosophic distinction: 'unlike Semitic religions, God is not an external commandment for us, but resides within ourselves. Our religion teaches us to realize this divinity progressively within our lives. This is supposed to impart to Hinduism a quiet, introspective, non-intrusive character.'8

Already we are on the way to an invisible slide which insidiously takes us to a very different plane. The very love and tolerance that is associated here with Hinduism must place it above other religions which are then consequently relegated to a lower-order existence. Since these are defined by the absence of love, so the argument goes, they are made intrinsically intolerant, expansionist and violent. A whole range of characterizations grow from this point, spelling out danger that needs to be resisted. Hindu tolerance is always counterposed against supposed Muslim intolerance and fanaticism, relying on the unstated and unproved assumption that the philosophical postulates of a particular religion (which are in this case arbitrarily taken for granted) constitute the exclusive, unchanging organizational principles for an entire people across all kinds of spaces, times and historical changes. If Hinduism is more tolerant (which is stated as an axiom and is nowhere really expounded) then all Hindus at all times will be peace-loving. Whatever the provocation, since Islam is a proselytizing religion, all Muslims are necessarily intolerant, so the argument goes, whereas a Hindu Rashtra is a safe repose for all creeds and sects. A Muslim-majority India, or a secular state which takes Muslim support into account, must be dedicated to the conversion of Hindus and to turning India ultimately into a fanatic Islamic state which will root out all other beliefs. In our investigations at Nizamuddin, the VHP, Arya Samajist as well as Sanatan Dharmist, insisted that this was going to happen in three distinct ways: Muslims, being irrepressibly and aggressively lustful by nature, rape Hindu women and force Hindu wombs into producing Muslim progeny; their legalized polygamy enables them to breed at a great pace, so that the existing Hindu demographic majority is a fragile and vanishing reality and Muslims will soon outnumber Hindus. The project will be aided by the influx of Muslim money from the Islamic countries and invasions from Pakistan. All three arguments have been extensively developed by VHP journals and pamphlets. In fact, they have become the received wisdom even among a large set of middle class, urban, educated people who do not otherwise subscribe to VHP programmes. The corollaries to these assertions (each is made without concrete reference to historical or demographic evidence, or when this is done, the source of information is conveniently missing) are significant. The secular state, which is part of the conspiracy, must be replaced by a Hindu Rashtra to ensure real toleration. Toleration, to be secure, must then stamp out all that is not Hindu, for what is not Hindu is always intolerant.

Bhandari and Sudarshan both ended their expositions on Hindu tolerance with shrill diatribes against Islamic 'expansionism'. Dr. Saifuddin Jeelaney's interview with Golwalkar[9] includes a quip by Guruji who had apparently been told by a 'tolerant' Sufi that the only path to religious unity was conversion to Islam. The moral, therefore, is that even the best of Muslims is a fanatic. Similarly, Seshadri *et al.* conclude their hitherto reasoned description of Hindu tolerance with: 'The Muslim is not prepared to give any right to people other than his own Muslim sect,' and the Christian is equally bad. Hinduism is under a ban in Nagaland, they declare. 'Even the pseudo-secularists are more fanatic and intolerant of any other idea of so-called secularism.' The 'Western' origin of other political and religious faiths are thus given a racial cast which makes their 'violent intolerance' a characteriological trait. To this is added a conception of colonial discourse and power-knowledge, which allegedly induced self-forgetting among us and imposed alien categories of understanding, structuring a false self-knowledge. The West conquered us by its own form of knowledge, while the Muslim had subjugated us through 'brute force'. As an example is cited the very notion of communalism itself, which is called and classified away as a colonial category.[10]

Emphasis on Hindu pluralism permits yet another slide—the

Hindu must fight the 'intolerant' Muslim so that the intrinsic tolerance of Hinduism may remain in command. We have seen its political implications in riot situations. The Muslim is represented as a danger because he (or the Christian or the secular) does not subscribe to a homegrown religion unlike Buddhism and Sikhism. Having first assured explicitly that the Muslim is an equal part of the Hindu nation, an unannounced, silent move is slipped in and non-homegrown religions are made simultaneously alien, anti-national and threatening. The move is reinforced by a parallel one. Savarkar's definition of Hinduism was an overtly 'secular' one, linked to devotion to the Holy Land alone, but then land was immediately sacralized through a Hinduization of its geographical, historical, even zoological features. Golwalkar had prescribed a shared 'respect for the cow' as the only basis for Indian unity whereas Seshadri describes a true Hindu home as a space sanctified by domestic shrines and holy icons, and a Hindu disposition as marked by regular temple attendance, daily worship and, at least, 'minimum *samskaras*'. like naming, marriage and funeral ceremonies.[11] Having first been freed from all observances, the Hindu is then thoroughly reinvested with all the known marks of orthodox Hindu piety. At the same time, the celebration of complete freedom and plurality of choice transforms itself into a series of observance, of 'musts', of the very external commandments which are supposedly the marks of non-Hindu Semitic cultures.

All persons outside these boundaries are not Hindus, i.e., not Indians, and can therefore only function as potential or actual traitors. There are, however, ways of separating out 'bad' from 'good' Muslims. After all, even Rithambara had made a distinction between 'Babur ka aulad' (children of Babur) and 'Rahim ka aulad'. Vaman Das Agarwal, (retired Professor) elaborated this point in a VHP publication entitled *Hindu Rashtra*. 'Those people are also included in the Hindu society who were forced to become Muslims and Christians, i.e., those who see their faith as a mark of conquest, not as a genuine conviction.' The VHP does take some pains to present us with evidence of their presence. The bulk of the hate-filled *Angry Hindu*, for instance, is written by Sikandar Bakht. One of the 'charioteers' of Advani's *rath* was a Muslim. The moral drawn from these instances is that those who do not share this opinion are simply perverse. Uma Bharati gave a very literal expression to this moral in her speech at the Delhi Sant Sammelan in April 1991: 'Muslims always do the opposite of what Hindus do. If the East is sacred to the Hindu, then the Muslim will worship the West.'

Within the imagined Hindu Rashtra, the Muslim is first declared a free and equal citizen and then his survival is made conditional upon a number of criteria imposed by Hindus alone. This seems to be so far the most substantive content of the notion of Hindu Rashtra. The *rashtra* (nation) is conceptually separated from the state and is defined as a cultural idea which embraces a community that resides upon a piece of land with which it shares an organic as well as an emotional relationship. The sacred significance of the land is central, since Savarkar's definition of the Hindu serves several functions. Through it, a continuity with the structures of feelings of nationalism has been retained. The Muslim remains forever the symbol of those who disrupted this sacred integrity and divided this holy land. Both associations are carried over into a struggle for Ram's land, and it is important to remember that the general implications of the RJB movement are mirrored at micro levels in a number of Hindu-Muslim land disputes. Similarly, 'we-ness' (Seshadri *et al.*) which seems to be a carry-over from the idea of '*chiti*' (integral humanism) must assume a condition of permanent struggle with the 'non-we' other, since the identity of Hindus cannot be pinned down to any other commonly accepted denominator. The practical embodiment of this essential 'we-ness' is a supposedly continuous, commonly-held body of *dharma* which has always summed up the laws of Hindus. In actual history, however, different Hindu sources had described this *dharma* in very diverse ways. By refusing to spell out particularities, modern Hindutva is absolved from restricting itself to any concrete or known rules.

While the nation remains undefined and amorphous, something of the general shape of the desired state, however, can still be deduced. 'Democracy' and 'secularism' (which must be in full consonance with Hindu Rashtra), are recommended, though very occasionally and somewhat perfunctorily. It is also generally qualified with many reservations. *Integral Humanism* had already identified democracy as a Western notion, which breeds problems. The cautionary note was strengthened by Sudarshan and Bhandari, both of whom expressed a firm commitment to an absolutist state, within which the individual must learn to merge his/her identity. Desires must always be collective, otherwise they turn irresponsible. The principle of the harmony of the whole was invoked each time, to confirm the necessity for complete submission of the individual parts.

Centralization is complemented with a predilection for a totalitarian, big-state complex. Girilal Jain, whose book *Secularism versus Nationalism* (first published serially in the RSS newspaper *Panchajanya*) starts with a glowing description of the King-Emperor or Chakravartin, who not only ruled the whole country but who also continuously expanded his territories. There are longing references to India's supposed rule over Afghanistan, Sri Lanka and Burma. Empire building was obviously the high water-mark of Hindu glory.

The conjunction of the *Arthashastra* and the *Manusmriti* in VHP discourses sums up a highly stratified, rigidly hierarchized ideology of the state and the domestic sphere.[12] While the *Arthashastra* describes a highly organized surveillance system, complete monarchical and bureaucratic controls and monopolies, the *Manusmriti* advises on how best to rule over the subordinate spheres of Shudras and women.

The supremacy of the family over the individual is reinforced by the gender ideology of Hindutva. The *rashtrasevikas* implied that family considerations should reign supreme in marriage and career choice, and that even organizational work must depend on family sanction. Seshadri asks Hindu NRI mothers not to opt for professional careers and glowingly describes how a senior bank officer-cum-VHP activist in the U.S.A. has given up her job, to bring up her children better. NRI teenagers are issued strong warnings about miscegenation which ultimately implies severe parental control that would distance the NRI youth from Western modes of intersexual sociability. Through carefully-regulated marriages within the high caste-upper class NRI circles that the VHP bases itself on financial resources are concentrated within the community and are not dispersed beyond its boundaries. The business interests of a commercial class which rely on Hindu norms of conjugality were expressed in a very different context, too. At Khurja the RSS *sanghchalak* referred to Sita's chastity and its influence on true Hindu wives. It was only the certainty that Sita's precepts are being followed that enables traders and businessmen to go away on long business trips with an untroubled heart. Seshadri provides an inventory of Western social and moral flaws: they range over widow remarriage, divorce, adultery, drugs and 'sexual orgies' without distinction. The Hindu man triumphs over the Western man in his ability to regard all women, except his wife, as mothers. Interestingly social and domestic purity is made more actively dependent on controls over male sexuality rather than on the woman's whose chastity is more or less taken for granted. The RSS exaltation of the ascetic model (segregation of shakhas, celibacy of sarsanghchalaks and of most pracharaks and pracharikas) marks an important distinction between itself and other similar patterns for youth organization. The fascists and the Nazi youth fronts had inculcated a hard macho attitude and an aggressive male sexuality. Here however, the ascetic Brahmanical model attempts to temper the virility of the warrior ideal, and contains it within a frame of low key, monogamous, chaste manhood which carefully regulates its sexual activities within strictly procreative purposes.

One of the most sinister features of recent Hindutva has been the highlighting of the militantly communal woman in a variety of unprecedented ways. A certain disjunction is noticeable between the continued austerity within the Rashtrasevika Samiti and even in the domestic ideology of new Hindutva, and the flamboyant militancy of the new woman activist of the Hindu Right. Rural women at Bhagalpur in 1989 or upper middle class Maruti-driving women at Ahmedabad in 1991 have appropriated active roles on the centre stage of riot scenes where they would rarely put in an appearance before—an ironic inversion of the woman's traditional invisibility. According to VHP reckoning (which was conveyed to us at their Ramakrishnapuram Office at Delhi in February) 20,000 kar sevikas courted arrest on 4 January alone at Ayodhya, and a total of 50,000 were involved in the entire December–January round of satyagrahas. The VHP fortnightly, Hindu Chetna of 15 December 1991, displays a cover photograph of kar sevikas sporting the saffron headband. The caption says: 'Matrishakti ka Abhyutthan'. Its Ayodhya office is selling works by women poets, like the Shraddha Suman Mala, which celebrates sacrifices by mothers and wives of martyrs. *Amar Shaheed*, a VHP account of the October/November events, accords particular importance to Vijayaraje Scindia's arrest. If 'Kaalchakra', a Hindi video news-magazine, focuses long and pointedly on the victim figures of a lone woman resister being dragged away by the police on 30 October, then the woman as a dynamic leader is highlighted by the 'Newstrack' (covering October events) where Vijayaraje Scindia is striding purposefully between two senior and enormously respectful police officers towards a car, from inside which she is shown again as leaving messages for the future conduct of the movement. VHP office-bearers in Delhi spent a long time explaining animatedly to us the precise differences in the quality of speech between Uma Bharati, the BJP MP and Sadhvi Rithambara, a *'sanyasin'*. And finally, and most obviously, if Advani and his *rath* had been the visual emblems of Ram Janambhoomi, then the voice and the words that fixed its message belonged to a woman.

Nor is the phenomenon a flash in the pan. The BJP has located women along with SC/ST as a primary target area for the next elections and, for the first time, has formed a new group of full-time women cadres to work for them. The new scenario definitively demolishes a rather comforting article of faith that prevails among certain groups of feminists: that women are intrinsically a force against communalism and that they are victims, healers, preservers of community memories during and after riots, but not its active agents.

Admittedly the Hindu communal groundswell has been restricted largely to urban U.P., to predominantly high caste, middle class milieus, as even VHP activists admitted to us. At the same time, the strength of the new phenomenon must not be underestimated. *Kar sevikas* have been mobilized from traditionally the most conservative backgrounds—upper class, middle ranking service sector and trading families. The very limits of the movement may then be taken as signs of strength within a different kind of reading. Nor can we draw false comfort from any illusion that these women are not speaking their own minds or their own words. While speaking to a bunch of male *satyagrahis* at Ayodhya, we were for some time faced with an array of archaeological-cum-historical arguments as well as the standard RSS definition of Bharat as *'pitribhumi, matri-*

bhumi, punyabhumi and *karmabhumi*'. Then Chandravati, a woman from Aligarh, excitedly broke into the conversation and introduced a very different note: *'yavan aye hain khoon barsane ke liye...mandir ka arth mulla ko phansi lag jaye...Mulayam aur VP ko phansi lag jaye'* (we have come here to shed blood...the meaning of temple building is that *mullas* should be hanged, Mulayam and VP should be hanged). The whole discussion was subsequently shifted to a markedly more violent plane. Nor does it mean that women voiced mere mindless abuse. Each of the *kar sevikas* interviewed—VHP as well as non-affiliated ones—played a distinctive individual variation on the themes of Ram Janambhoomi and Hindutva. For Vijaya Dube, a would-be *sanyasin* from Ghaziabad, Hindutva implied a sweeping, millenarian vision of collectivity (*samashti*) *'Yeh (Hindustan) samudra jaise gambhir hai, aakash jaise vyapak hai...Hindu hi adi ant hai.'* (It is as deep as the ocean, as endless as the sky...the Hindu is the beginning and the end.) Unlike other religions it is not time-bound but eternal. It is not an individual but a collective experience. It finds its centre of gravity in Ram Janambhoomi which then becomes: *'hamara sarvaswa hai, dharam ki bat nahin hai, sarvasarvaswa hai'* (it is everything to us, it is not just a matter of religion, it is our all, it is our everything). With the liberation of Ayodhya, *'poora vishwa badal ho jayega, ek naaya shrishti ka nirman hoga'* (the whole word will change, a new creation will come into being). For Mithilesh Vashisht, a VHP worker from Modinagar, on the other hand, the value of the movement lay in the assertion of strength and self-respect against oppression: *'atyachar, anyay naahin sahenge, kisi cheez ki seema hoti hai'* (we will not tolerate oppression and wrongs, everything has limits). Another (unidentified) woman intervened with a more poetic-mythical version of the necessity: *'yeh hamara ang hai, hamara abhushan hai...Krishna bhagawan ka chakra hai'* (this is a limb in our body, an ornament...it is the chakra of Krishna). All *kar sevikas* were bursting with speech—with arguments and descriptions, each had an accent very distinctively her own. Within an as yet limited social and geographical scope, then, the Ram Janambhoomi movement seems to have effected major breakthroughs in women's political self-activization, not available to earlier communal upsurges.

In a curious way the present movement inverts the usual pattern of symbolization within national and earlier communal movements. So far, in both, the fetishized sacred or love object to be recuperated had been a feminine figure—the cow, the abducted Hindu woman, the motherland. Here, however, the occupied *janambhoomi* belongs specifically to a male deity, and women are being pressed into action to liberate it and restore it to him, to bring back honour to Ram's army of monkeys and squirrels has now acquired a new combatant and Sita's sex is coming to the rescue of Ram—an inversion of the epic narrative pattern where Ram and his army had to go and bring Sita back. The reversal of roles equips the communal woman with a new and empowering self-image. She has stepped out of a purely iconic status to take up an active position as a militant.

In this context, the very careful and significant handling of the baby *Ramlalla* image acquires new meaning. Ayodhya stalls sell a large number of stickers and posters depicting a chubby infant baring his pink gums in a toothless smile. Local legend has it that in 1949, just before the deity 'miraculously' reinstalled itself within the mosque, a police constable had found a dark and lovely child playing by himself in that corner: the homeless baby had come back home to claim his patrimony. The VHP video cassette produced by J.K. Jain, 'Bhaye Prakat Kripala', reproduces the event over a long time. We must remember that Ramayana and the *Ramkathas* resonate with the many losses of Rama: he loses his kingdom, his father, he is separated from his mothers and his brothers and then he loses Sita—his is a figure bathed in tears, a reason perhaps why the common man and woman can identify more with him than with other mythical heroes. The entire series of deprivations has now been collapsed into the shape of that irresistible human idol—the deprived male infant. On top of that, within the mosque and next to the main deity, is an icon of the crawling *Ramlalla*—a posture traditionally associated with the baby Krishna and linked to a long chain of associations with emotional and aesthetic structures. While the appeal of the homeless baby would be a general one, it would be especially poignant for women. Readings of recent events that insist on a monolithic militarization of Hinduism by present iconic trends, therefore, miss out on their *versatility* which is their most remarkable feature. While the *Ramlalla* appeals to the mother in

her, the warrior Ram probably simultaneously arouses a response to
an aggressive male sexuality.

All this, it needs to be emphasized, is a rather new development.
The presence of women was minimal even on the crucial days of 30
October and 1 November. At the Rashtrasevika Samiti office we
were told quite frankly that the decision to train *kar sevikas* was the
result of an internal debate that was eventually won by younger
Samiti members. VHP news-sheets that covered the *shila pujan* and
shilanyas ceremonies of 1989 gave little scope for the women's voice.
Even Rithambara's cassette addressed its invocations to rise and
fight exclusively to men: *'bir bhaiyon jago!'* (brave brothers awake!)
Women listeners were obviously being targeted as well. There were
intimate references to domestic politics among mothers, sisters and
daughters-in-law, to women's work within home. Yet the call to
action was addressed each time to brothers: 'you have to make your-
selves into a clenched fist, my brothers.' Inspirational feminine examples still related to motherhood: Bhagat Singh's mother, crying
after his death, not because she had lost her son, but because she
had no other son to be martyred. Even the Rani of Jhansi was
invoked as the mother of a brave patriot. The warrior figure of a
queen as the adversary of Babur was inserted into the 'Bhaye Prakat
Kripala' video cassette, and Sadhvi Rithambara and Vijayaraje Scindia were endowed with an exalted position at the climactic phase
of the Ram Janambhoomi movement. But they were, still, excep-
tional, rare figures: women in general remained the productive
womb, mothers of heroes. The flood of ordinary *kar sevikas* thus
represents a very recent shift, pregnant with possibilities for Hindu
communalism, as well as with problems.

Yet linkages do exist between the austere, deliberately self-lim-
iting pattern of work of the Rashtrasevika Samiti and the current
tumultuous militancy. There has always been a primary emphasis
in the self-definitions produced by the Samiti on physical courage
and strength, on a trained, hardened, invincible female body. *'Swasangrakshanksham nari ki samaj me adhik pratishta hoti hai'* (a woman
who is able to defend herself gets a higher status in society), declares
a Samiti publication. The specific deity which sums up their aspirations is the militant icon of *ashtabhuja* Durga who subsumes Saraswati, Lakshmi and Kali. *Sevikas* are meant to meditate on her

weapons particularly. They see themselves as full-fledged soldiers in an impending apocalyptic war: their daily pre-meal *mantra* is translated as: 'our limbs and bodies have been nurtured by our motherland and we must give them back to her in her service alone.' Why is a strong feminine body of such primary importance? Expounding on this theme, Asha Sharma, who is in charge of the Delhi organization, explained that this binds up the notion of sacrifice with that of active fighting. When I asked if it was some kind of a civil war situation that she had in mind, she replied that it was a possibility. Certainly then, the explicit purpose for which the empowered Hindu female body is trained is patriotic war against the Muslim combatant. The large place that the myth of Muslim lust occupies within the general mythology of Hindu communalism would also explain the need for self-strengthening. Yet we must remember the oral version, the origin myth of the Samiti—Muslim criminals raping a girl in the presence of her Hindu husband—and also the reference to the larger status of the *'swasangrakshanksham nari'* (a woman who can defend herself) within her own social milieu.

Defence against and respect within her own environment is then the implicit subtext which might, in everyday calculations, become a more powerful motive force and a more real compulsion than the ultimate political intention of *Hindutva jagaran*. When we consider the context from within which the Samiti mobilizes and trains its women, the force of the immediate compulsion becomes clearer. *Sevikas* come from upwardly mobile, urban, solvent, trading or middle-ranking service sectors—a fertile breeding ground for dowry murders and the violence on wives that precede them. Women's organizations that deal with huge numbers of divorce or maintenance suits arising out of this social level, are very familiar with the violence and oppression that flourish here against women. In the big northern cities, if not in the rich small towns so far, education and professional opportunities for women have come in late and recently but have come in a big way. Nor are families opposed to women's employment and professional training since it is regarded as a valuable source of extra income. Thrust into public and mixed spaces for the first time, women encounter yet new forms of overt or covert sexual discrimination and violence. It is no wonder that the physical training programmes of the *shakhas* prove extremely

.ttractive to such women, with the promise of a powerful body and
he attendant self-confidence. That body and that mental attitude
hat it generates would be a vital shield against gender oppression
vithin domestic as well as public spaces.

We may then assume that despite the overarching aim of Hindu
>ower, the woman needs also to utilize Samiti facilities to empower
1erself against her own hostile environment. Problems of the newly
mobile professional women are often discussed in the *Jagriti*, the
Samiti journal. An article, for instance, describes how the author
vithstood the offensive behaviour of a police officer who partially
undressed himself in her presence when she had gone in to report
a street accident. Several others take up this theme: how to construct
a responsible and fearless woman-citizen and teach her to exercise
1er civic rights and duties within a chauvinistic world.

Two very different readings of the precise location of the Hindu
woman within her own society seem to be jostling each other within
the Samiti. The *Pramukh Sanghchalika*'s speech at the 1990 annual
conference insisted that '*Bharat* (read Hindu) *ki nari sarvada se mukt
hai*' (the women of India have always been free). An article in *Jagriti*,
entitled '*Rashtra ka adhar nari*' reiterates this conviction and traces
a long history of her power within Hindu society from Manu to the
current movement. Yet the same issue carries another article—*Nari
Jagaran*—where the present women's movement in India (which is
not equated with the specifically Hindu movement) is described as
a result of and an antidote to the generalized oppression against
women. Whereas the earlier trend is extremely critical of the global
women's movement as a sign of Western corruption, the latter ex-
plains and legitimizes it. Another article, '*Parivartit parivesh me Bharatiya nari*', criticized Indian men for obstructing the larger entry
of women into politics. It is interesting to see that while the more
authoritative statements—Golwalkar, RSS strictures, the Samiti's
official accounts—applaud the new Hindu women for resisting
Western modernism, women's own articles, when they deal with
their everyday problems and perceptions, are little concerned about
Westernized modernity. In fact the new Hindu woman citizen is
sometimes cast in a mould which is very close to that of bourgeois
feminism. '*Nari ke sarvangin vikas ke liye uska arthik roop se swatantra
hona paramavashyak hai, atah nari ki arthik swatantrata ke liye rozgar*

me sanghrakshan hona chahiye tatha usse sambandhit sabhi mukaddaamo ke liye mahila nyayadhish chahiye.' (In order to attain the comprehen sive development of women it is extremely important for them to be economically independent. So, in order to ensure economic inde pendence, they need reservation in employment and they need women judges to conduct all cases related to such issues.) The new Hindu woman is therefore a person with professional and economic opportunities, secure property ownership, legal rights to ensure them and some amount of political power to enforce these rights.

Women's power is a theme that is evoked and celebrated, often in the most grotesque of circumstances. At the Ayodhya *kar seva*, a crowd of women was chanting the beautiful feminist slogan: '*Hur bharat ki nari hain. Phool nahin chingari hain.'* (We are the women of India. We are not flowers, we are sparks.) When our interviewe asked them why Sita was absent in the invocations to Ram, the men fell silent but women had their answer ready. One said that this was Ram's birthplace and not Sita's which accounts for her absence But Vijaya Dube interrupted her to say that Shri actually means Sita and hence in the chant 'Siya Ram', Sita is actually placed before Ram. The interviewer asked, 'You mean Sita is contained in Ram? 'No,' said Dube, 'Sita comes before Ram.' Not only has though gone into the location of Sita, there was also a recognition that Sita must come before Ram. In a VHP book for children, *Hanuman k Kabaddi*,[13] Hanuman declares himself to be neither Ram's *bhakt*, no Sita's *bhakt*, but the *bhakt* of Sitaram together.

And yet it would be utterly wrong to suggest that a sort of women's liberation is going on happily within a somewhat unfor tunate Hindutva framework. They offer no formal legal counseling to women, nor is divorce encouraged. Dowry is regarded as an evil yet there obviously is no ban against its practice among RSS o Samiti members. If a demand for full citizenship rights and affir mative action is made in *Jagriti* from time to time, there is no critical review of Hindu patriarchy. When *kar sevikas* at Ayodhya were asked if their status would improve within Hindu Rashtra, one of them said yes, because Muslims then would not be allowed to have four wives and that alone would ensure greater respect for women. She could not, on the spur of the moment, think of any other possibility within Hindutva for herself. While the Durga

Vahini mobilizes young women exclusively for agitation by trans-
forming religious discourse into a sustained hate campaign, the
Matri Mandal has stuck to its limited, low key programmes—im-
plying an intended gap between the nature of expectations from
young and older women. Yet, once they have gone through a more
activist orientation, it is likely that the same lot of girls might find
the role model for older women irksome.

Just before the mid-term elections in May 1991, some women
activists publicly interrogated spokespersons from major political
parties about their programmes for women. Malkani, the BJP
spokesman, was most often at a loss and found very little to say to
the women. He also infuriated a lot of labouring women from slum
areas by chastising them for bringing their babies into the hall. 'Are
our babies shoes and slippers that we can leave them outside?' they
retorted.

If gender represents a problem area for Hindutva, so ultimately
does caste. Hindutva claims to have abolished caste within its realm.
The caste of *shakha* members is not mentioned in admission forms,
and, within *shakhas*, apparently there is no way of telling the caste
composition. 'I want to strike out the word "caste" from the dictio-
nary,' declared B.L. Sharma with much heat. *Sant sammelans* regularly pass untouchability removal pledges, and Manish Chaudhury,
a Bajrang Dal student from Aligarh told us that the RJB movement
was created 'to organize Hindus and remove caste'.

Distinctions need to be made, however, between somewhat vague
strictures against the caste system as a whole and far stronger verbal
exhortations against the specific practice of untouchability. We also
need to distinguish between verbal exhortations and the concrete
absence of any involvement with Dalit struggles. While theoretically untouchability is excluded from the classical Hindu social
model, the caste system itself is covered with silence. We find many
positive references to the principle of *varnashram dharma* with the
routine proviso that it does not validate untouchability and that it
aspires to a system of mutuality. We were told that the *shakha
bauddhik* sessions never raise any discussions on caste since it might
make the lower caste members sensitive. On this ground therefore,
any critique of a problematic theme, that could have interrogated
the RSS vision of a unified Hinduism, is avoided. An anecdote

recounted by a *rashtrasevika* also contradicted a previous assertion that the caste of members remains unknown. She said that she had to break a ritual fast and accept tea from a harijan *sevika* to convince her that she did not believe in untouchability. Clearly the caste affiliation of the harijan member was known and as a harijan this *sevika* harboured a suspicion of discrimination.

In Delhi, we (i.e., a group of visibly Westernized, 'secular' people) had talked to national level leaders of the Hindu Right. They were quick to size us up and pronounce a RSS-VHP version of social order which would be most acceptable to us. In small towns and rural areas, however, our 'liberal breed' with its anti-caste values is a relatively unknown element. Local level leaders were consequently far more open in their talk. At Bilhaur and Unnao in central U.P., RSS volunteers working in villages candidly admitted that their organization depended on upper castes. Chakravarty Awasthi, RSS *pracharak* and BJP activist from Teesti village (near Bilhaur), admitted that *shakha* members were drawn mainly from traders. Just before the 1991 elections we had found a highly articulate awareness among lower castes about the upper caste complexion of the RJB movement. A group of lower caste villagers openly accused Sudulhare Awasthi, an important RSS activist of Bilhaur, of promoting the RJB movement and of disrupting normal business in order to speculate on grain prices. At Khurja, Bhardwaj, ex-President of the BJP and a teacher of English literature at the local NREC College, described the BJP as a 'middle class, upper caste' party. Bhagwan Swarup Bhayya, the RSS *sanghchalak* of Khurja whose family owns considerable interest in crockery and cloth business, described the *shakhas* as catering to students and businessmen.

A major feature of 80s' politics has been the catapulting of the OBC sections, especially the Yadavs, into political pre-eminence in the two crucial states of Bihar and U.P. Their insistence on a corresponding share in educational and job opportunities strained a system which, since Independence, had guaranteed implicit upper caste dominance in the key, interrelated sectors of political governance, administration and business. The failure of the Congress to appropriate their demands created an ideological crisis in 'mainstream' politics. While the Congress 'consensus' that had in effect been complicit with upper caste domination started to come under strain, there was corresponding consolidation among the upper castes to face this new challenge in new ways. It was Hindutva with its militant unified Hinduism that offered a counter thrust to the OBCs while disguising this with its public disavowal of caste.

While the Mandal proposals accelerated this process of upper caste consolidation, it did grievous harm in general to the Hindutva cause. It not only pulled back substantial groups of lower castes by highlighting an issue incommensurate with the image of unified Hindutva: much more importantly, it made it imperative for the RSS-BJP-VHP at the ground-level to take up the upper caste cause with some demonstrative effect. In the conditions of upper caste paranoia unleashed by Mandal, they would have had to lose much of the crucial upper caste support unless they made themselves visible in anti-Mandal demonstrations. At Khurja, Professor Elhance of NREC College and a BJP activist led an anti-Mandal demonstration which was disrupted by stone-throwing harijans. Elhance suffered injuries on the head. After the Bhagalpur riots, a VHP ideologue had told a visiting PUDR (People's Union for Democratic Rights) team that OBCs in the Hindu belt had been marked out as the target of their attention. Mandal largely put paid to such visions of mobilization through Ram and through minimal charity work.

At the VHP rally in Delhi on April 4, a slogan that came up from the floor was 'jis Hindu ka khoon na khola, woh Hindu nahin, woh bhangi hai' (those Hindus who haven't shed blood are not Hindus, but of the sweeper caste). A Maharashtrian Brahmin journalist told us at the rally that he had joined the VHP to rectify 'Hindu hurt'. He defined this as the appeasement of lower castes at the cost of 'poor Brahmins'. A Hindu Jagaran Manch leaflet published from Khurja reiterated the same charge. Khanna Lal, a farmer-cum-shop-owner from Binki village, Fatehpur, U.P., attending the VHP rally described his village Yadavs as predominantly farmers. As soon as he said that the crowd around him began to shout, 'No don't say they do farming, say that they do loot mar (criminal activity).' At that rally we were told by every group we met that harijans and OBCs had come in great numbers. No group, however, could provide actual evidence of their presence. Incidentally, there was a striking absence of contingents from the North-East or Hill areas as well. Large groups of RSS activists had come from Hyderabad, but they admitted that all the speeches at the rally were in Hindi and that they could not understand them. They also admitted that there was only one temple dedicated to Ram in their city and that was a very new one.

As with caste, the VHP-RSS track record reveals no sign of involvement with class struggles. We found no discussion of rural class struggles let alone an involvement in such issues. S.K. Varma, Secretary of the BMS (Bokaro Majdoor Sabha) Union at the Bokaro Steel Plant, told us that they opposed strikes on labour demands since they destabilize the national economy. The VHP leaflet— *Warning: India in Danger* referred to strikes as a sign of communist treachery against the nation—especially among 'railway workers, bank employees and *karmacharis*'. The only strike the BMS had engineered in Bokaro was in 1965. According to Varma, it was only ostensibly about greater safety measures for the worker on the factory floor. The real reason was a show of BMS strength to undercut the importance of other unions. Yet another reason was an attack on Bindeshwari Prasad Dubey's government. The BMS motto is, '*rashtrahit* first, *mazdoorhit* second'. *Rashtrahit* (welfare of the nation) is identified with *Hinduhit* (Hindu welfare), and the BMS receives regular postal instructions from the VHP. Political leaders of the VHP addressed workers within the union office on RJB. Yet, curiously, even the working class politics of the Hindu Right seemed to have a distinct discipline of its own: 'We never invite *sants* to our office, only political leaders,' Varma told us.

The BJP has several ways of tackling this social dilemma. Once the militant moment of its movements was over, and the anti-Mandal storm subsided, it reverts to its ritual gestures towards Harijan welfare—notably in U.P. where it has seized power. It also preserves its ascendancy over lower castes without undertaking any meaningful reforms in their status through a monopoly over ground-level intellectual leadership. Even where it has no direct bases among lower castes, it exerts an ideological influence through teachers and priests. Mitra Sen Yadav, the CPI ex-MP from Faizabad, made to us the important observation, that harijans and OBCs have not so far thrown up their own intellectual leaders. Bhardwaj at Khurja indicated yet another resolution of the problem of a basically upper caste base and ideology. This was located within the traditional caste structure of Hinduism and its endless self-divisions. There cannot be a sharp polarization between upper and lower castes to seriously threaten BJP ideology, for the low castes maintain strict ritual divisions among themselves. Referring to the relative purity of the better educated Jatavs over other harijans from whom they do not accept water, he made a revealing statement: 'A Jatav hates a harijan more than a Hindu hates a harijan.' Clearly he was seeking solace from the fact that harijans are far too stratified to challenge the overall hierarchical scheme of caste. At the same time, the Hindu here is admittedly someone who is not a Jatav or another kind of harijan i.e., he is an upper caste person. The Hindu is also *bound* to hate the harijan, even if the Jatav hates him more.

Perhaps the most important answer to this problem of social limitation without undertaking any fundamental change within internal power arrangements, is the device of rioting. In 1983—the year of the VHP's foundation in Khurja—there was a brief conflict between Valmikis (an upwardly mobile section of Bhangis), and Muslims in the town. The pattern was repeated on a much enlarged scale in the riots of December 1990 and February 1991. In BJP-VHP-RSS narratives, riots seem to be confined to Muslim versus Valmiki conflicts. Upper caste Hindus are depicted as sympathetic onlookers rather than as active protagonists. No doubt, part of the strategy is to secure their own line of retreat, by finding themselves convenient and dispensable scapegoats. Valmikis have been deployed in similar communal conflicts—in Nizamuddin in 1983 and in the walled city riots in Delhi in 1987, for instance. A more fundamental motive, however, seems to be the Hinduization of this upwardly mobile section from among the Bhangi caste through the test of rioting for Ram's cause. They are given the privilege of fighting for Ram—a privilege that would incorporate them within a spiritual brotherhood without upsetting the material status quo. Similarly, a Harijan was given the great privilege of laying the first foundation stone at the temple site in 1989. Symbolic solidarity is expected to overshadow the necessity of practical solidarity. In fact the VHP promotion of the Valmiki group in particular, is significant. It coordinates with Valmiki temple committees for its festivals. VHP literature pays obeisance to Valmiki and Ravi Das as

Hindu religious leaders. The association between Valmiki and Ram
is striking, It is also significant that in Delhi, Valmiki temples
abound and constitute practically the only visible monumental activity from among low caste groups.

We have dwelt a great deal on the upper caste/class composition
of Hindutva. In conclusion, it should be observed that this social
group has changed its character. In the 80s there was a tremendous
boom in both the numbers and prosperity of this upper caste/class
formation which was bred in great part by the upsurge in consumerism, fuelled by imported screwdriver technology and facilitated
by 'soft' bank loans and government-aided small scale industrial
projects. Predictably this has led to widespread and rapid social
mobility. Simultaneously, the base for a huge civil and military
bureaucracy has grown, spanning urban as well as semi-rural areas
in north India.

It was (and remains) a class that was committed to two objectives: to an unfettered growth of consumer capitalism and to a
strong state that could manage the political crises of the country
and the economic discontents arising from the boom in private enterprise. For a time, this class found its representative, indeed its
self-image, in the person of Rajiv Gandhi and his policies. His
political ineptitude in addition to the internal crises within the
Congress, paved the way for Hindutva—with its aggressive right
wing world-view embodied in a seemingly coherent ideology, its
emphasis on a strong organization together with the projection of
itself as an untried party to acquire the allegiance of this class.

THE MEDIA

When we began our work on the Nizamuddin riots in April 1990,
we had found that the VHP was focusing on the production of
printed literature, leaving audio-visual messages largely to the care
of the Doordarshan authorities—a proof of which lay in the contro-
versies surrounding TV serials: the "Uttar Ramayan" serial to follow
the "Ramayan", demands for the ban of "Tamas", debates over the
serialization of "Tipu Sultan". In an incredibly short time, however,
the situation changed drastically. By about August 1991, VHP cul-

tural production was predominantly audio-visual—the Jain Studios video productions, 'video raths' and Rithambara's audio cassettes. Other political parties have also attempted to exploit the media boom in our country which started from the late 70s, and in fact, the pioneer here had been Rajiv Gandhi. But today the RSS-BJP-VHP network has far outstripped other political tendencies so far as media manipulation is concerned.

Moreover, the VHP uses the media in a distinctive way. Political parties and individuals, such as Rajiv Gandhi and N.T. Rama Rao, used the media for electoral purposes alone (though the government did promote a new view of India's past, as we shall see). On the other hand, the VHP broadcasts a vision of Indian history extending to the present. Using all the media techniques at its disposal—dramatic sequences, editing, music, commentary, etc.—it tries to project its world-view as the natural source of this country's heritage. This in turn naturalizes the RSS-BJP-VHP claim to be the legitimate representative of Indian historical aspirations and needs. The persuasive power of these media products should not be underestimated. For instance, Advani in his speech in the April 4 rally in Delhi, referred to the VHP videos to prop up his claim that there had been a massacre in Ayodhya. He did this despite the repeated revelations published in *The Sunday Observer* and *Frontline* among others, which have established that many *kar sevaks* classified as dead by the VHP are actually alive, with many of them never having gone to Ayodhya at all. Given this persistent persuasiveness of media technology that enables these leaders to make claims contrary to public facts, it is important to decode the ways in which the VHP uses images to communicate its own messages, and understand the implications of the particular social and political programme that the VHP is pushing through their naturalizing presentation.

Much of the VHP's power in being able to present its world-view as natural is due to the impact of the televised "Ramayan" serial. The VHP cassettes do not have to spend time to popularize the "Ramayan" nationally: on the contrary, they can build on the themes that the serial had outlined. Ramanand Sagar's "Ramayan" projects Ram's life and character as a national ideal. The VHP develops this dubious point by indicating that Ram's heritage has reappeared through the 'rebirth' of the baby *Ramlalla* in Ayodhya in 1949.

The focus in 'Bhaye Prakat Kripala' (hereafter BPK), the first of the VHP video cassette series, is on the sacred land that is Bharat, with Ayodhya as its capital city. Bharat, the narrator assures us, was gifted with superior wisdom by the Gods, which was embodied in Ram. The visuals dissolve from a simulated shot of the cosmos to a clearly defined, saffron map of *'Akhand Bharat'* with a blinking light showing Ayodhya, to suggest that India as a geographic entity was born with Ram. Ayodhya then becomes the heart of the body of Bharat. After quickly relating Ram's tale, the video turns to Babur's invasion, so that its abrupt entry suggests a sudden violence wreaked on the undifferentiated being of Bharat/Ram. It is now that the people of India came alive, led by innumerable rulers and *sadhus* who waged repeated battles against the invaders. The already stirred memories of the serial are now given a concentration and new direction by images of Muslim barbarism: a miniature of a Muslim slaying a deer suggests the perversity of their violence, while their continuing and looming menace is created by a short, inflammatory sequence showing shadows of knives on a street wall. On the other hand the counter-movement is shown in the 'rebirth' of Ram, who is pictured with a bow and arrow which he points to the audience with a seductive smile. Ram, the narrator had told us earlier, was the 'desire and identity' of Bharat, and extending this principle, baby Ram is given the familiar look of a sugary 'Glaxo baby'. Ram is thus presented as a contemporary ideal by translating him into the idiom of commercial advertising icons.

What is the idea that emerges from this presentation of Hindus and Muslims? On the one hand, pre-Mughal history is forgotten in the mythology of Ram. This gives the impression that the Hindus had never had any differences among themselves, or with other religions and cultures; nor do they seem to have developed their own society and culture after what the gods had gifted them. By making Ram embody Hinduism, it makes the latter a finished product and puts an end to the prospect of any further development of Hinduism itself. On the other hand, the Muslims do not seem to have any other aim except the humiliation of Hindus. There is no suggestion of the human aspirations lying behind Islam, the vastness or the diversity and richness of the Indo-Islamic cultural heritage. In fact the Muslims are robbed of their humanity and manipulated by these cassettes to demonstrate the need for Hindu mobilization under the banner of Hindutva. The Muslim, for Hindutva, is only an instrument.

Two elements characterize the VHP presentation of Hindu mobilization. Firstly, they show it as a spontaneous stirring (a *jan jagaran*) and correspondingly they play down the role of the actual mobilizing agencies, the RSS and its affiliates. BPK shows the Ram Janambhoomi movement as emanating from *dharm sansads* (at Delhi and Udipi) and other meetings of religious heads held at Ayodhya itself during the *shilanyas* programme. In these meetings traditional feelings of reverence attached to religious discourses are given a political and activist direction. The speeches of these religious leaders have little to do with explicating religious texts and ideas: different *sanyasis* give different messages, ranging from Ram's national identity to the innate secularism of Hindu *'dharm'* and to the need for a militant mass movement etc. In their saintly garb, these religious personnel actually mouth snatches of the entire RSS-VHP programme while the immense number of speakers gives the impression that traditional Hindu leaders are doing so spontaneously. In these proceedings, the organizations other than those of *sanyasis* occupy a subordinate position: the leadership of the VHP is shown to be primarily in the hands of Mahant Avaidyanath, who makes the important announcements. The RSS is presented as if it were yet another religious organization by locating it among these leaders, but its position is made memorable visually by inserting the absent Deoras's image in golden outline, while his message is read out. The position of the RSS is made more ambiguous by presenting it repeatedly as an organization that is engaged in drills and marches—clearly suggesting a more long-standing source of contemporary militant Hindutva than the platform of *sanyasis*. Following a pattern noted earlier, the guiding hand of the RSS is simultaneously concealed—and subtly displayed.

Strangely, by the time we come to the last cassette in the VHP series 'Pran Jaye Par Vachan Na Jaye' (hereafter PJP), the *sanyasis* are only seen, but not heard. We hear only the non-religious leaders of the VHP. The change can be seen in the shift of leadership from

Mahant Avaidyanath to Ashok Singhal, who is also a man of action. He is the first wounded person we see on the screen, and thereafte a stream of the dead and the wounded follow, giving the message that even in violence and adversity Singhal remained the leader. On the other hand, the *sanyasis* function either in a ritual capacity chanting *mantras* and preparing the *shilanyas* ceremonies, or are used as images to heighten (sometimes indiscriminately) the sense of outrage at police action.

We had earlier referred to the way in which the VHP cassette inhumanely strips the Muslims of their humanity. This instrumentalist approach to the 'other' community is also ironically evident in the way the VHP makes the *sanyasis* subordinate to the RSS leadership symbolized by Ashok Singhal. Hindutva is quite prepared to use the Hindu religion as a pure instrument for its own self-advertisement—and it tries to do this in a way that seems naturally a part of a spontaneous movement.

The image of Hindus as spontaneously moving to recover their lost inheritance in the Ram Janambhoomi, needless to say, hides the careful planning and political aims of the RSS-BJP-VHP in preparing this movement. But it also does something equally dangerous. It defines Hindus as people who fulfill themselves in violent action—which makes a mockery of Hindutva's professions of commitment to democracy. As we have observed, the *sanyasis* do not engage in discussion: they merely mouth the RSS programme. And the 'people', as we shall see, act only as violent 'inspiration', clearly dispensing with the value of debate or dissent. Hindus, for the VHP, are spontaneously authoritarian.

The image of crowds (besides the shots of meetings) in BPK is that of rustics who sing a steady, unexcited *bhajan* as they walk along. By the time we come to PJP, this is transformed into a wild and violent storm, led by youths with *lathis*, flags and *trishuls*. This 'spontaneously' violent crowd is then shown to organize itself into a determined, collective congregation on November 2, which inches its way in a stubborn block towards the *masjid*. All this while of course the effect of the mobilization is seen as widespread: women actively help either by pouring water to neutralize tear gas, or if they know English, by pressurizing the district authorities; a rustic leaps in joy and grabs hold of an equally enthusiastic urbanite as

96

hey walk along the city streets (incidentally offering a magical olution to the contemporary resentment of farmers against the ity). This seemingly autonomous development of Hindu militancy evelops from an inexplicable energy, and in this parallels the magical power of Ram to 'reincarnate' himself in 1949

By giving political violence engineered by the VHP the religious anction of Ram, it demands that the viewer should be obliged, in he natural course of things, to be violently communal. It tries to nake it incumbent on the viewer to join other Hindus in their sacrifice' and 'awakening'. It may be remarked here that these cassettes attempt to build up a tremendous pressure of frustration and nger, by repeatedly dramatizing the Hindus in a victim role. The Hindu warriors and religious leaders generally fall a (heroic) victim o the Muslims. It is significant that a 'successful' Hindu warrior ike Shivaji is not mentioned. And yet ironically, the truth of such n intense presentation of Hindu victimhood and continuous Hindu hurt' throughout history, is belied by the tremendous resources which the VHP has accumulated and deployed, a wealth that is vident in the slick programming of these videos, and the extent of heir distribution. In many, many cases, these cassettes were distributed free of cost!

The call for violence is also structured into the very way these assettes arrange their sequence of audio-visual images. It is intersting to see how these productions mask their call to violently onfront the secular state, when it is ostensibly giving a different message. Sometimes, as it narrates a particular event, a sequence, ymbol or any other element from some popular film is inserted, which when added to the sequence being shown, gives it a different, mplied meaning. Thus the video cassette 'Ramji Ki Sena Chale' was meant to capture a peaceful rally that flagged off the BJP's electoral mobilization, but it manages to project this as a continuation of the militant Ayodhya campaign. The opening shot presents a human Hanuman, climbing the raised platform that overlooks the main podium. Meanwhile the soundtrack reproduces a portion of the signature tune of (ironically enough) the TV serial, "Tipu Sultan", which is a wavering, bugle-like sound that immediately precedes the long shot of Tipu and his army marching to battle. The reference to the militaristic "Tipu Sultan" soundtrack gives to the

97

chant of 'Ram rajya ayega' a combative edge, enables it to represen
the April 4 rally as virtually a declaration of war on the India
secular state, without however committing itself to any clearcu
position that might invite legal prosecution or alienate the less mil
itantly inclined amongst potential voters.

Elements of mass commercial entertainment are used by th
VHP-BJP to both mobilize and keep alive a sense of participatio
when the movement is not going through its dramatic moments
'Ram rajya ki ore chale', an election campaign videocassette, has th
BJP programme presented by Archana Puran Singh with small skit
enacted by TV stars Vikram, Rita Bhaduri and Lakshman of th
"Ramayan" serial fame. Mass meetings themselves become a sourc
of entertainment news; on April 4 the famous commercial musi
director Ravindra Jain released a new song composed specially fo
the rally.

The idiom of commercialized mass entertainment has enabled th
organizers of Hindutva to popularize traditional religious institutions also. In our visit to the Jhandewalla Mandir in Delhi, w
encountered the amazing spectacle of a *bhajan* session which feature
a band that had a saxophone, an electronic keyboard and drum
topped by a look-alike Amitabh Bacchan crooner. The mood in th
congregation was a far cry from the serious rapture of *bhajans* o
yesteryears: there was loud laughter as the singer, in an act tha
recalled stock Hindi film scenes, held out the microphone to a littl
boy in the audience while encouraging him to sing with the background music. Most of those present were women, and the congregation seemed designed to release them from their everyday
schedules through a community formed by the joy of 'live' entertainment even when it was ostensibly gathered for a serious, religious objective.

Besides women, popular music is also targeted at the youth.
'Ram ki nam le', a cassette available in Ayodhya panders to the
cinematic ideal of youthful romantic love. It makes Sita play the
seductive damsel calling out to Ram in a tune which imitates the
hit song *'Dil diwana bin saajana ke mane na'* with the following
words, *'sone ka mrigaya le kar Raghuvir ao na'* (come to me Ram with
the golden deer). Besides making Ram function like a film hero,
the VHP music cassettes also seek to encourage an activist disposi-

tion, which elsewhere they define as the prime characteristic of youth. 'Chalisa aur 6 December', for instance, has three tracks of recitative liturgy to the tune of *Jai Jagdish Hare* backed by brass organ and drums, which gives way to a catchy tune that creates a carnivalesque atmosphere, in which the lyrics urge the killings of V.P. Singh and Mulayam Yadav!

Popular media culture has been so thoroughly internalized by the organizers of Hindutva, that the movement itself has become a source of entertainment. It involves a double victory for the VHP. The boom in video cassettes has allowed it, through its own productions, to create an alternative to the Congress monopoly over Doordarshan. On the other hand, the increasing autonomy of Hindi film music from the film itself (the song *Dil diwana* was a hit long before the film, "Maine Pyar Kiya" was released), offered an opportunity to create political pop without necessarily reminding the audience of the actual context of the film itself, which besides being jarring may have also had a comic effect. In this way Hindutva has attempted to become as familiar as common sense.

Among the most powerful facilities of new media technology is its instant amplification and easy transportability. These features have been used recently in western U.P. in amplified cassettes playing sounds of riots from cars that vanish without a trace, leaving in their wake an actual riot. The absence of any visible agency coupled with the blanketing effect of amplified sound is designed to create a sense of paranoid isolation for the minority community, which would encourage them to cling to violent self-defence as the only guarantee of security. Further, the possibilities of amplification are used by the VHP to include the individual listener in a collective sphere of illegal activism without disturbing his/her social position and comforts. 'Chalisa aur 6 December' which contains a terroristic message, explicitly warns the listener that he would be infringing the law if it was listened to.

The riot-noise cassettes broadcast an image of a fictitious riot, that in fact results in a new one. In fact, many of the VHP's media products appear to possess a self-fulfilling function. For instance, Sadhvi Rithambara's cassette talked of the necessity of a huge 'once and for all' battle, which was borne out by the later events in Ayodhya. In turn the Ayodhya incidents can be read back into the cassette to confirm its truths when Rithambara talks of the conditions of Hindu 'persecution' in a secular state, and the heroic resolve of the Hindus to liberate the *janambhoomi*. This cassette then becomes a kind of superior historical authority which by its ability to 'read' the future, confirms its largely fictive interpretations of the past. This ability to 'see' the future is no mystical operation. What it does reveal is the close coordination between the aims of the movement and the media message. Rithambara's cassette, it must be remembered, was released in order to mobilize support for the *kar seva* in Ayodhya.

By preserving and replaying the human voice and the spoken words, the audio cassette achieves an impact qualitatively distinct from the one resulting from re-reading a text. The latter also can grow and acquire new meanings in overtone, but it remains an individual exercise, a private act. The spoken word is addressed to a whole congregation and proceeds through a continual interchange of passion between the speaker and the listeners. New technology is able to recapture that exchange *ad infinitum* for freshly or differently constituted congregations, and, at the same time, allow the first message to fatten on new meanings and associations gathered from the movement unleashed by itself, grow from its own self-fulfilling prophecies. Rithambara's words on martyrdom would have had a much enlarged and transformed response for people listening to her cassette after 30 October.

Rithambara's voice circulates with the ubiquity of a one-rupee coin in north India. Rithambara has in the process become the first mass leader in our country, who has been created by a recorded cassette: she has herself become an extension of that cassette, for all her highly successful public speeches draw upon its format. But more than drumming up support for particular movements, this cassette has generalized and intensified communal attitudes to the point that they have become the meaning of existence for many. In his parting words, the Pesh Imam of the Babri Masjid implored us to do something about this cassette, for it, above all, had destroyed completely the affective basis of their relationship with their Hindu neighbours: 'ek nafrat ki deewar khadi kar di. Hum aaj bhi milte hain, magar dil saaf nahin hain' (it has built a wall of hatred: we still meet, but our hearts are no longer pure).

Possibly the most important feature of the Rithambara cassette is the voice. An hour long harangue without any modulation, high-pitched, breathless, taut with intensity, at its shrill moments appearing to break down with the strain of humiliation, the voice is at once outraged and hectoring, it has the immediacy of an address on the field of battle. Technology covers its own traces so completely here that we forget that what we are listening to is recorded speech—and not a live recording of an actual speech either, but a studio artifact which with meticulous deliberation and coordination has pieced together over long stretches a carefully rehearsed address. The greatest success of technology it may be observed, lies not in preservation or duplication, but in its naturalizing abilities, its self-effacement. Rithambara's cassette is thus an appropriate embodiment of the whole RSS-VHP technique of presenting a highly orchestrated and controlled movement as natural and spontaneous.

But the voice has more to it than pure intensity, which after all could become wearisome. In some ways the form of presentation in the Rithambara cassette is reminiscent of the *Ramkatha* tradition, where the speaker selects a single line from the *Ram Charit Manas* and extends its *bhava* (mood) by citing different folk sayings, scriptural injunctions, snatches of devotional songs, coming back repeatedly to chant lines from the book itself.[14] Rithambara's voice is obsessively focused on the theme of violent confrontation, but it does give the audience moments of reprieve from the high tension, by slipping into stories (which range from the mythological to the domestic), or couplets which while modulating the mood, nevertheless reinforces the basic messages and prepares the listener for a return to the battlefield spirit.

While the form of presentation gives traditional religious practice a communal objective, thematically, Rithambara recharges communal prejudices with a new energy and direction, using terms to explain the contemporary experience of post-Independence India. The most significant feature of her indictment of the secular state is its corruption. Her own position as 'sadhvi', one who has apparently renounced worldliness, provides her with the moral justification to launch an all-out attack against the post-Bofors world of Indian politics. In this India everything—honour, honesty, courage patriotism—are for sale. And nowhere else, it is implied, is the commercialization of political character more evident than in the refusal to build the Ram temple, a denial that is compelled by the fear of losing Muslim vote banks and foreign cars. A supreme example of successful market manipulation thus becomes the launching pad for a denunciation of commercial corruption. Ultimately however, as the Pesh Imam's words suggest, the everyday burden of this violent morality falls upon the Muslim. Though the battle with the Muslims is rendered as a heroic battle in the past with the children of Babur and Aurangzeb, the figure of language used to describe this is 'tu, tu, main, main' which in Hindi is synonymous with a no holds barred contemporary street brawl. In fact Rithambara's battle situation is assumed to be an everyday occurrence. Thus most Muslims in India, according to her, cunningly tolerate *mandir* bells where they are weak, but initiate riots where their strength permits. The only way a Muslim can redeem himself is if he adopts Ram as his ideal. An example of this 'good' Muslim is shown in BPK in the figure of a Muslim havildar who ecstatically relates how the baby *Ramlalla* suddenly manifested himself in Ayodhya in 1949, thereby concealing the actual communal force used in implanting the idol. By bringing together anger against State corruption with the evocation of street violence against the Muslims, Rithambara's cassette finds an ideal solution for the casual problems that plague any movement against the State. These have their ups and downs and the intensity cannot be maintained on an everyday basis. But because the living Muslim occupies the social sphere, anger against him would be seen to keep alive the fight against the state. The power of Rithambara's cassette lies not least in the fact that it finds a simple, accessible target, violence against whom can mean for the Hindu, a magical liberation from the bondage of an immoral system.

An outstanding success of the VHP's media policy has been its ability to influence the 'independent' media, especially during the Ayodhya *kar seva* days. We compared two video news reports on Ayodhya in Hindi and English, produced by 'Kaalchakra' and 'Newstrack' respectively. The 'Kaalchakra' programme is entitled "Voter or Leader?" and it proceeds to unfold a report in which the *kar sevaks* (representing the 'voters') are pitted against the then political leadership—a story structure that is derived from the general

VHP understanding. While Advani the leader of the 'voters' is shown in his full personable self in conversation with the interviewer, Mulayam Yadav is represented as reading from a prepared speech. Imitating the PJP sequence (see above) the camera takes him from the ground with a special lens, exaggerating and caricaturing his action so that he emerges as the stereotype of a non-human, non-serious puppet politician. There are other straightforward imitations of the VHP production, for instance, the Muslims are introduced by a hunting image. Having established the masterful, violent character of the Muslims, it goes on to show them in a mosque, which, drawing on another stereotype, identifies the source of Muslim power in the seemingly more organized nature of their religion. The next sequence is of *kar sevaks* shouting *'Jai Siya Ram'* and laying bricks. Their aggressiveness is thus shown as a necessary answer to Islamic perversity, while the VHP by being given a status on par with Islam itself, emerges as the sole representative of the Hindus. Finally, after dramatizing the 'outrage' at Ayodhya by focusing on *sadhus* being beaten and women being dragged, it ends on a note of celebration with the screen freezing on a still shot of the Babri Masjid with the soundtrack relaying the slogan *'lathi golee khayenge, mandir wahin banayenge'* (we will face sticks and bullets, but we will build the temple there).

'Kaalchakra' presents its report in the way the VHP would like to see it, as describing a religious and cultural movement. 'Newstrack'—which is more concerned with the expectations of the more 'liberal' minded, managerial middle class, sees it as a political movement spun out by a responsible BJP leadership in order to counter the Mandal issue (as contrasted to 'Kaalchakra' where the BJP plays a minor role). There is thus a great deal of focus on how this movement has been mobilized (from the *Rath Yatra*) in an organized way, while the capability of the leadership is shown in the image of Vijayaraje Scindia leaving messages for the future conduct of the movement as she is being escorted away following her arrest. At the same time, some hard questioning of BMAC (Babri Masjid Action Committee) leaders which stops at the question as to whether Babur had not committed a wrong in building Babri Masjid, extends to the Ayodhya movement a measure of moral support on this issue. Nevertheless, compared to 'Kaalchakra' there is not much intensity, little by way of celebrating popular outrage. On the other hand the unsettling aspects, the fact that it seeks to alter the way this country has related to itself, are pruned away in the general message that this movement like any other, is simply a continuation of the old politics in a new style.

It can be claimed with good reason that no report is free from bias, but the VHP seemed to have so intensively influenced the independent media, that the latter's reports had little to do with the factuality of events. The climactic point in fictive reporting coincided with the assault on the Babri Masjid. The Ranchi edition of *Aaj* dated October 26, 1990, carried screaming headlines, claiming that the Ram *mandir* had been destroyed, while the report only stated that the canopy over the *shilanyas* pit had been removed. Inspired by Rithambara's cassette, the Patna edition carried a poem that called V.P. Singh a progeny of Jai Chand and compared him to Ravana. On November 2, a special bulletin of *Dainik Jagaran*, carried a double column item claiming that a Shri Ram Kranti Brigade would cut off the hands and feet of Mulayam Singh by the following month. The Kanpur edition of *Aaj*, on November 3, proclaimed through its headlines that Jalianwalla Bagh faded into insignificance when compared to the Ayodhya killings, while the Bareilly issue of November 1 frankly advised readers through its headlines to come armed to Ayodhya, adding that V.P. Singh and Mulayam Singh should be thrown to the dogs. The *Swatantra Chetna* of Gorakhpur found a novel way of confirming the wildly exaggerated figures of the dead. In the special bulletin of November 2, it had published the figure as 15. However at the last minute a 1 was inscribed by hand to make the total 115.

Clearly this amounted to deliberate disinformation, and not merely misreporting. The process of large sections of the press (especially Hindi)) becoming mouthpieces of communal mobilization, is, in retrospect, not a sudden development. There was an established bias in riot reports against the Muslims, most dramatically revealed in the inadequate coverage of brutalities inflicted on the Bhagalpur Muslims, and in spotting a fictitious Pakistani hand in the riots. On the other hand, once the *Rath Yatra* started there was little coverage of any of the riots that it left in its wake or the general sense of insecurity if generated amongst minorities. By

October 1990 however, newspaper reports started to play a direct, active role in initiating riots, and not merely explaining or sanctioning them. A typical instance was the *Aaj* report on the 'demolition' of the Babri Masjid with a photograph of the Ram *mandir* printed alongside. Once this was circulated in Ranchi, mobs set fire to Muslim shops, attacked mosques and killed at least two people belonging to the minority community. In Aligarh, a massive round of bloodletting was sparked off by the publication of a wrong report that Hindu patients were being killed in Aligarh hospitals.

The English language press with its more cosmopolitan readership and 'liberal' self-image, was also biased in its reporting. Thus Hindutva's projection of the *Rath Yatra* was adopted wholesale. The crowds who came to greet the *Rath Yatra* were seen to be motivated by religious devotion. The fact that it was a political venture, that the 'Ram devotees' who flocked to see Advani were instigated by and largely composed of RSS and BJP workers, the general wave of insecurity it created amongst the minorities. These facts were either absent or suitably played down while reporting. On the other hand, through editorials and signed pieces, newspapers such as *Indian Express* and *The Times of India* sought to provide intellectual legitimacy. For instance, in a series of articles, former editor of the TOI Girilal Jain excused Hindutva's violence as Hindu backlash which he perceived as a minor reaction to Muslim fundamentalism. All the while he propagated the VHP world-view (which he was also explicating in the RSS organ, the *Panchjanya*) through the pages of his English newspaper.

The intensity and spread of this press mobilization for Hindutva was clearly unprecedented in post-Independence India. What was then responsible for this? A possible explanation for media activism after August 1990 can be found in the anti-Mandal agitation. A recent study[15] has shown how newspapers deliberately played down news of riots while they highlighted news about the anti-Mandal agitation: for instance, between August to September 1990, *Indian Express* devoted 1281 times as much space to the anti-Mandal agitation than to the riots. This is not merely a question of interest alone, the anti-Mandal agitation led directly to the support for the *Rath Yatra* to enable it to bring down V.P. Singh's government.

What is alarming is that at moments of extreme pressure, such as the anti-Mandal agitation and the Hindutva movement, dissenting voices are given an extremely subordinate position in newspapers, if at all. A possible reason for this degree of orchestration is the change in patterns of newspaper organizations, which have in recent time been marked by the intuition of big business investment and the growth of a corporate culture which has tended to centralize the internal workings of the profession. In Maharashtra big companies such as Larsen and Toubro or Bisleri, which have promoted Shiv Sena labour unions to oust existing Left labour unions, have been among investors in newspapers whose reports have sometimes sparked riots.[16] On the other hand, since the beginning of the 80s there has been an organized attempt by the RSS to infiltrate the media. The consequences of this infiltration were visible during the Ayodhya days. According to the Press Council report on the newspaper coverage of the Ayodhya events, it is said that many editors behaved as if they were part of the Ayodhya movement. It is alleged that one of them used his press privileges to smuggle in Ashok Singhal, another editor was seen directing *kar sevaks* while many had participated in VHP rallies and had given provocative speeches. Finally the system of employing 'stringers' (part-time reporters) at the local level has added to the wave of misreporting. Stringers generally lack expertise, are given low wages, and have a social background which has contributed many cadres to the Hindutva mobilization, consisting of contractors, dealers, shopkeepers, lawyers and local petty leaders. According to a report in the *Economic Times*, many *mahants* of local temples in Ayodhya acted as stringers.

The extent of networking between Hindutva and the media may be surprising, but the fact itself is obvious in retrospect. The larger question still remains: what has happened to the relationship between media, society and politics in our country that could provide a sanction for such a widespread broadcast of utter untruths?

A brief consideration of elements that were (and still are) produced outside the interventions of the Hindutva organization, could help us in some way, in answering this question. One was the growing preoccupation with the image of this country in the international arena starting off with a big investment in the ASIAD Games of 1982, and crystallized nearly a decade later in the holding of international exhibitions presided over by Pupul Jayakar, which sought to wipe out the image of India as a poor and conflict-ridden country by emphasizing the ethnic richness of its heritage. The preoccupation with the living conditions of the poor was converted to a glamourization of the products of folk culture. In a country that was internally going through major conflicts which ranged from socio-economic issues to questions of regional autonomy, this celebratory image of national pride became important for both the state and the middle class, for it permitted association with the poor, but silenced their contemporary aspirations. Together with this must be considered the other element, that of contemporary religiosity. The widespread success of the religious-mythological films of Bombay had to an unprecedented extent removed the cultural products of religion from religious institutions themselves, and reassembled in cinema halls the congregations that would normally gather in temples. A major development occurred in the mid-seventies, with the release of the film "Jai Santoshi Ma" which proved so successful that in some cases, driven by devotional enthusiasm the audience threw coins on the screen as offering. More than anything else, this film created a whole new, popular, near-national religious cult. Further, the importance of popular entertainment in revitalizing religion became evident in the mushrooming of *jagarans*, which were generally financed by shopkeepers, and where the words of traditional *bhajans* were recast in popular film tunes.

A growing preoccupation with the image of the nation when its society was undergoing its worst crisis in the post-Independence years on the one hand, and the ability of the mass media to appropriate and contemporize the rooted traditions of devotion into easy, attractive and dramatic images without entering too much into theological debates or the way different sections of people related to religion on the other, were the two strands of image-making brought together under Rajiv Gandhi in the serialized "Ramayan". This programme reduced Hinduism to its mythology which was then presented as the essence of nationhood. The images of national pride could be served more effectively by the mass popularity of devotional traditions revolving around Ram, something which the dabbling in sports and ethnicity lacked. Finally this potent mix was broadcast from a monopoly holding that assembled a grand national congregation by beaming it into every household or community centre at a fixed hour every Sunday morning.

In this serial the story of Ram is shown to be a unifier of the diverse traditions of the country: even south India—where the Ram legend is hardly popular—is shown to be sharing as passionately in the myth of Ram as the north. Ram's story is also said to have spread internationally (including Iran and the U.S.S.R.) proving that a global hegemonic role is possible for India, if she rallies together. The moral message that is said to account for the power of Ram's story is one of courage against oppression. It is a morality that is not very different from the one that has preoccupied the Hindi screen from Raj Kapoor to Amitabh Bacchan. Yet there is a fundamental reversal of the Bombay film theme. The source of oppression is not within society as occurs in Bombay productions: the oppression comes here from Ravana, an outsider to the just, Aryan society represented by Ram. Thus there is no need for society to change: it only needs protection. Cinematically this just society is brought into the present tense; for instance, the celebrations at Ram's birth resemble a Republic Day parade featuring folk dances, images that suggest the Indian State today can claim to be just, for it is of Hindu descent.

But the central feature of the serial is Ram himself, a figure meant not only to be revered, but to be emulated. When the baby Ram cries, Shiva tells Parvati that though he is an *avtar*, Ram has to behave like an ordinary mortal so that human beings can model themselves on him. In keeping with this Ram is obedient (he carries out the decisions of the Gods), moderate (never given to the excesses of the rebel hero of Bombay films). In short, Ram embodies all the virtues that would remove dissent and debate within society. And yet Ram's *raison d'être* is a violent cause, and the serial constantly suffuses the audience with the martial theme. Even a bathing scene of women turns to a discussion of the Kshatriya body. But Ram's violence is of a modern kind: he releases an array of hi-tech weapons. Ram is also a technocrat, who is more concerned with organizing violence than with indulging in it himself. This image of Ram is reinforced by a major emphasis on the training he undergoes as a child, while little else of his childhood is shown: a clear departure from Valmiki and Tulsidas's versions. Of course this training is received in a *gurukul*, which only goes to re-emphasize the point that technological knowledge is far from being incompatible with Hindu pedagogy. Even though the serial catered to mixed audiences, its most noted triumph was marked in annexing the upper middle class urban youth, with no moorings within Indian realities, to Ram's cause. *Sanatan Dharm* leaders, as well as Arya Samajist ones from South Delhi, reiterated this point in their interviews with us.

The serialized "Ramayan" gave to the brand new phenomenon of high consumerism and media technology imported by Rajiv Gandhi, an immediate culture together with a sense of rootedness. It provided to the new aggressive social class spawned in the 80s a packaged, collective self-image which, with the mobilizing by Hindutva, became the motivating force for changing, by force and violence, the image of the country itself.

NOTES

1. Our account of the Nizamuddin riot follows in a second monograph. See also Pradip Datta, Biswamoy Pati, Sumit Sarkar, Tanika Sarkar and Sambuddha Sen, 'Understanding Communal Violence: The Nizamuddin Riots', *Economic and Political Weekly*, 10 November 1990.
2. *Charcha ka Vishay: Mukhya Sutra*, RSS booklet, Delhi.
3. For an account of the extent of charity-oriented work of the Hindu right in Madhya Pradesh, see Christopher Jeffrelot, 'The BJP in Madhya Pradesh: Networks, Strategies and Power' (unpublished article).
4. See also Seshadri, Sudarshan and Madhok, *Why Hindu Rashtra?*.
5. See for instance the RSS booklet, *Charcha ka Vishay: Mukhya Sutra*, or Ananda Shankar Pandya, *Relevance of Hinduism in the Modern Age*.
6. See Ram Swarup, *Hinduism vis a vis Christianity and Islam*.
7. See *Rakt Ranjit Itihas*.
8. Ram Swaroop, *op. cit.*
9. Saifuddin Jeelaney, *Shri Guruji on the Muslim Problem*, Suruchi Prakashan, 1971.
10. *Spearheading National Renaissance*, RSS publication, Karnataka, 1988.

11. Saifuddin Jeelaney, *op. cit.* Seshadri's *Hindus Abroad: The Dilemma— Dollars or Dharma*, Suruch Prakashan, 1990.
12. Chandar Mehra, *Understanding Hinduism.*
13. *Hanuman ki Kabaddi*, a tract acquired at Ayodhya.
14. Philip Lutgendorf, 'Ram's Story in Shiva's City: Public Arenas and Private Patronage', *Culture and Power in Benares: Community, Performance and Environment 1800–1980*, ed. Sandra B. Frietag, Delhi, O.U.P., 1989.
15. Charu and Mukul, *Print Media and Communalism*, Delhi, Mukul, 1990.
16. Charu and Mukul, *ibid.*
17. *Ibid.*

4

Conclusion

The Hindu Right, particularly in its present incarnation, is engaged in fundamental forms of religious engineering—and this is where its political agenda differs most significantly from other right-wing formations. The distinction between Hinduism and Hindutva, between traditional religiosity and its perversion by communalism has, therefore, been asserted often enough. In such polemics, however, religiosity is equated with a rather static, textual or anthropological view of practice and belief. Along with politico-economic changes, the contours of Hinduism as practised by the urban and rural middle classes of northern India (the present bases of Hindutva) have also been rapidly and visibly changing over the last two or three decades, providing a favourable context for intervention by the organized forces of Hindutva.

Even before the VHP came into its own, there was an upswing in certain new modes of worship and new sacred symbols. These included, among many other things, a proliferation of *jagarans* around mother-cults like *Jai Mata Di* in places more or less without such cults so far; a media-invented goddess like Santoshi Ma; devotional pop music; a rush to modern 'hi-tech' pilgrimages for the upper middle classes, like Vaishno Devi; and charismatic gurus or god-men, each with a distinct interpretation of Hinduism and salvational strategies for well-defined clienteles. With the growth in so many diverse forms of religiosity, why is it that among them it was the hard, communally-oriented, politicized brand of devotion

111

that has, at least for the moment, gained ground over others, appropriating quite a few of them?

The new forms of religiosity from the 50s and 60s coincided with a visible decline in the importance of traditional *sanyasis*, *sants* and *mahants* within the middle class milieu. Perhaps this accounts for the easy success of the VHP mobilization drive, investing them with renewed authority. Certain tentative connections may also be suggested between the growth of Hindutva and the specific patterns of north Indian city and small town development in recent years. The new urban middle class, spreading out fairly deep into rural hinterlands, has based itself largely on the rapid growth of relatively small industrial enterprises and an attendant trade boom. Government planning since the 70s has promoted small private industries through training, initial support, and bank loans granted on an individual basis. This new sector has achieved a significantly higher growth rate than that of the large-scale industrial units, whether public or private. The Green Revolution in parts of U.P. has increased rural purchasing power significantly, thus feeding into the boom in urban enterprises, consumerism and trade. These small-scale units flourish without the concomitant growth of an organized working class, since individual work-places are far too small to consolidate the labour force and enable effective unionization. The recent enormous growth of small towns has depended largely upon such developments. Even a metropolitan giant like Delhi is crucially dependent on these strata, as well as on the vastly expanded civil and military bureaucracy. Growth of this kind was accelerated under Rajiv Gandhi with the boom in 'screwdriver' technology.

In significant contrast to the cross-state kinship and caste-based credit and trade networks which had characterized earlier phases of Indian capitalist growth (most notably Marwari enterprise), the new middle class tends to be fragmented into smaller, more individual units. They are marked by intense internal competition, the steady pressures of new opportunity structures, ever-expanding horizons for upward mobility, and a compulsive consumerism that keeps transcending its own limits. The very pressure of growth is disturbingly destabilizing; the brave new world of global opportunities creates anomie and existential uncertainties.

The more reckless the concrete material fact of competition and fragmentation, the greater, perhaps, is the need for an image of shared anchorage and a theory of collectivity, for disciplined commitment to a system of values that would never, however, challenge the basic material interests and aspirations of these classes. New cults have therefore flourished and god-men are created, while the RSS *shakhas*, which had worked primarily among urban trader groups since the 1920s, remained highly relevant with their disciplined solidarity, routine actualization of brotherhood, and claims to a pure, traditional system of *samskaras*.

But more, perhaps, came to be needed. The relatively quietistic *shakhas* with their long-term character-building perspective had possibly reached a plateau by the 1970s. Militant rhetoric found little outlet in action, and there seemed small hope of dramatic political success: the BJP electoral performance reached its nadir in 1984. And, if the cadres of Hindutva needed a new activist programme, the social groups from which they came could not be entirely satisfied with *Jai Mata Di*, Vaishno Devi, or god-men. These were still too individualized, unable to convey a sense of intense solidarity and collective life. Organized Hindutva was able at this conjuncture to effectively insert the new, aggressive, Ram-centred communalism, which raised solidarity to a new intense emotional level through its inherent militancy. One of its major departures compared, say, to god-men cults, is the continuous invocation of a threatening 'other', with whom an endless war has been joined through the campaign for *Ramjanambhoomi*: for beyond Ayodhya looms Mathura, Benaras and the vista of around 3000 temples still to be regained. The promise of assured success provides an additional attraction. The Muslim 'other', despite the propaganda about its threatening presence, is in real life a minority, grossly under-represented in the bureaucratic, military, professional and business elites, while Hindutva can rely on complicity from many elements in the state apparatus. The court judgments about Ayodhya in 1949 and 1986, the PAC involvement in innumerable U.P. riots, the role of the TV serial "Ramayan", and the prominence of ex-army men and retired civil servants in the VHP and BJP today are just some illustrations of these crucial linkages.

In fact, Hindutva has enjoyed a productively ambiguous relationship with the Indian state and its official ideology of nationalism.

The Nehruvian project had already sought to consolidate and institutionalize the nationalist self-definition of the newly liberated country into the preserve of a bureaucratic and over-centralized state dominated by its Hindi heartland. While the pressures of regionalism increased from the 60s to the present day, the process of centralization also continued, till a point was reached when merely belonging to the Nehru family became an instant criterion for national leadership. A consequence of this was the increasing turn towards appealing to Hindu sentiments to find new ways of legitimizing itself. The lack of success of such a political trajectory for the Congress has benefited Hindutva, which panders to the desire for centralization by propagating an ideology that bestows a single identity on the country, while it attacks the Congress for encouraging fissiparous tendencies and corruption, which have, in fact, been the result of over-centralization. This allows Hindutva to project itself as an oppositional and untried alternative to the Congress, while drawing on the very basis of what it attacks.

We have been exploring interconnections to discover the emergence of a conjuncture favourable for Hindutva. It is necessary, however, to guard against any slide into determinism. The conjuncture of the 1980s crystallized into today's powerful wave, not automatically, but because an ideological formation had emerged already, over a long process of historical development which we have tried to trace in outline. This formation, again, is far from being free of contradictions and inadequacies, and opportunities still remain for effective secular-democratic interventions to block the thrust towards Hindu Rashtra.

The expansion of the Hindutva movement creates its own tensions between the disciplined core of RSS cadres and the new, motley yet increasingly assertive group of *sants*, *sanyasis* and fellow-travellers mobilized through the VHP. The RSS chief administrator of the Jhandewalla temple in Delhi, for instance, was quite dismissive about the temple *pujari*. On the other hand, a Rajya Sabha BJP member who is also prominent in the VHP, told us that the real problem was that the RSS did not entrust others with responsibility. Tension between the core organization and the expectations of its mass following take other forms, too: for example, the BJP government in U.P. cannot afford to move at quite the same pace as the VHP on the Ayodhya issue. Such differences in tempo may prove to be the undoing of Hindutva's politics. Punjab and Assam have shown how the politics of identity can breed ever-increasing extremism that fractures the control of its original leaders. The present tightly-orchestrated unity of the Hindu Right may well become increasingly difficult to maintain, while electoral reverses in Madhya Pradesh and Himachal Pradesh indicate that the image of a pure, incorruptible RSS-BJP can get quickly tarnished through becoming a ruling party. Already, in post-election, BJP-ruled U.P., the different components of the family have started pulling in diverse directions.[1] While the BJP is today the ruling establishment in U.P., it also needs to pander to a militant movement whose rowdiness in October 1991 at Babri Masjid raised doubts about the BJP's ability to administer law and order, and indicated the destabilizing potential of the lumpen wing of Hindutva. The RSS too shows signs of returning to a more flexible range of options and, as in 1984, considers dialogue with the Congress. The cohesiveness of the joint family is again under stress. Equally important, as we have seen already, are the contradictions within Hindutva ideology and its inherent social limits, which it tries to paper over with silence or double-speak.

A focus on internal tensions can at times be politically dangerous. It is easy enough to slide into hoping for eventual automatic collapse through internal contradictions. An active contest requires a vision of alternative movement. The experience of the national movement at its high points, as well as that of the Left, indicates that secularism strikes roots only when it ceases to be an abstract principle, however well-meaning, and becomes integrated with popular struggle on concrete issues.

Maybe it is instructive to record that even at this triumphal moment of Hindutva, a different kind of event has dramatized the presence of questions and energies which pose a fundamental challenge to it. Shankar Guha Neogy, the innovative trade union leader, was murdered in the BJP-ruled state of Madhya Pradesh. His death has been the product of his political effectiveness. Guha Neogy shared with many other radical activist groups functioning on very diverse fronts (class, gender, education, environment) a capacity to encompass within his movement a large array of everyday questions.

They ranged from trade union struggles to an anti-liquor movement that involved moral self-reform and amelioration of the woman's lot at home. In the process, the problems of everyday life and that of organized mass movements get inter-linked, encouraging participants to examine themselves critically in their different social roles and the consequent diverse ways in which they relate to power (becoming, for instance, masters at home and victims in the workplace.)

In their own way, these groups carry the battle into the enemy's camp. For Hindutva is an ideological formation that draws a great deal of its power from the use of stereotypes and symbols. Through them, Hindutva tries to make its constituency see the problems of power and powerlessness as a relationship between stereotyped communities. Hindutva thus avoids the problem of examining and confronting the ways in which the unequal distribution of power and resources pervades the larger society and everyday relationships. A creative left-wing response to this challenge, as Neogy's and others experiments indicate, can engage in varied struggles involving different relationships of power. The deepening awareness of the multiple identities that constitute any collectivity which this process implies, acts as a discouragement to think in terms of stereotypes and symbols that seek to simplify the problem of power and identity. The death of Neogy, as well as the living tradition of his and other similar movements, pose questions as to how such initiatives are to be generalized beyond a locality, and how, if necessary, they can extend the range of issues they pose. In other words, it leaves us with the problems of constructing an alternative culture of change.

NOTES

1. *India Today*, 30 November 1991.